The Teacher's Sourcebook for Cooperative Learning

Practical Techniques, Basic Principles, and Frequently Asked Questions

George M. Jacobs

Michael A. Power

Loh Wan Inn

CORWIN PRESS, INC.
A Sage Publications Company
Thousand Oaks, California

Copyright © 2002 by Corwin Press, Inc.

For information:

 Corwin Press, Inc.
A Sage Publications Company
2455 Teller Road
Thousand Oaks, California 91320
www.corwinpress.com

Sage Publications Ltd.
6 Bonhill Street
London EC2A 4PU
United Kingdom

Sage Publications India Pvt. Ltd.
M-32 Market
Greater Kailash I
New Delhi 110 048 India

Printed in the United States of America

Library of Congress Cataloging-in-Publication Data

Jacobs, George M.
  The teacher's sourcebook for cooperative learning: Practical techniques, basic principles, and frequently asked questions / George M. Jacobs, Michael A. Power, Loh Wan Inn.
      p. cm.
Includes bibliographical references and index.
  ISBN 978-0-7619-4608-3 — ISBN 978-0-7619-4609-0 (pbk.)
 1. Group work in education—Handbooks, manuals, etc.
 2. Teaching—Aids and devices—Handbooks, manuals, etc.
I. Power, Michael A. II. Loh, Wan Inn. III. Title.
  LB1032 .J34 2002
  371.3—dc21
                                        2002000152

This book is printed on acid-free paper.

10 11 12 13   10 9 8 7 6 5

Acquisitions Editor:	Faye Zucker
Editorial Assistant:	Julia Parnell
Production Editor:	Olivia Weber
Typesetter/Designer:	C&M Digitals (P) Ltd., Chennai, India
Cover Designer:	Michael Dubowe
Production Artist:	Michelle Lee
Illustrations:	Andy Jacobs, Crows Nest, NSW, Australia
Indexer:	Teri Greenberg

The Teacher's Sourcebook for Cooperative Learning

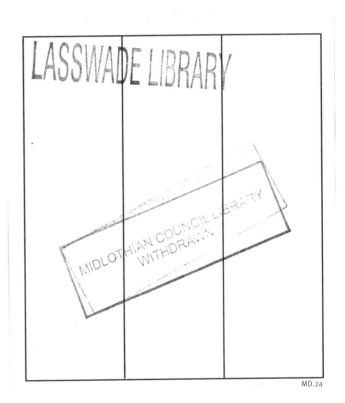

CORWIN PRESS

The Corwin Press logo—a raven striding across an open book—represents the happy union of courage and learning. We are a professional-level publisher of books and journals for K-12 educators, and we are committed to creating and providing resources that embody these qualities. Corwin's motto is "Success for All Learners."

Contents

Introduction

Lynda Baloche (1998) recounts that in her first days as a teacher, she quickly realized that students were much more interested in their classmates than they were in her or in what she was trying to teach. Lynda decided to use her students' fascination with their peers as a resource by introducing group activities. However, the success of these activities was hit and miss, and Lynda didn't know what she was doing right on the hit days or wrong on the miss days. Does any of this sound familiar?

A breakthrough came when Lynda started reading books and articles on cooperative learning (CL):

> I discovered that cooperative learning was what I had been trying to do. I discovered that there were basic principles that I could apply in my own teaching. I was excited. I was hooked. I was sure I could master it in about 6 weeks. (p. 2)

Well, it's now more than 25 years later, and Lynda has been using CL successfully all these years, in a wide variety of teaching settings. In fact, a few years ago, she wrote her own book on the topic (Baloche, 1998), and she's still learning!

WHAT IS COOPERATIVE LEARNING?

Johnson, Johnson, and Holubec (1993) define CL as "the instructional use of small groups so that students work together to maximize their own and each other's learning" (p. 9).

Our definition is similar: Principles and techniques for helping students work together more effectively.

The main difference in our definition is that by not using the term *small group*, we hope to emphasize that CL has value beyond the small group, a point that Johnson, Johnson, and Holubec most likely agree with.

The purpose of this book is twofold. First, we want to help teachers who are at the stage where Lynda was initially—who want to improve student learning and engagement and try some different ways to have students work together but aren't sure how. We will share eight key principles for facilitating cooperative learning in your classroom along with a variety of CL techniques and examples of how to use them. We call Part I of the book Getting Started With Cooperative Learning.

As Lynda realized, there's more than a lifetime of things to learn about CL. The second purpose of this book is to provide new ideas for teachers who have already started with CL. We look at a variety of issues and challenges that arise when we use CL. Over years of teaching our own students, using CL, observing other teachers doing the same, attending workshops and classes, and, later, training thousands of teachers—as well as years of reading and writing about CL—we have collected a wide range of ways to address these issues and challenges. We present these in Frequently Asked Questions, Part II.

We hope that teachers of all levels, from preschool all the way to university and adult education, and all subject areas, will find this book holds useful ideas on how the power of student–student cooperation can enliven their classrooms. Obviously, not every idea in the book will apply exactly as presented in every teacher's context, but we sincerely believe that the principles we offer have relevance to all contexts.

Three Windows on Peer Interaction

Deutsch (1949), in work expanded on by Johnson and Johnson (1998), has identified three windows through which students can view their peers—individual, competitive, and cooperative. Let's consider three students—Maria, Yan, and Ralph.

Maria looks at her peers through the individual window. She feels that whether her peers achieve their goals has no effect on whether she achieves hers, just like noncompetitive swimmers trying to improve their times.

Yan looks at her peers through the competitive window. She feels that what helps her peers achieve their goals hurts her, and what hurts them helps her, just like competitors in a tennis tournament.

Ralph looks at his peers through the cooperative window, believing that what helps them achieve their goals helps him achieve his, and what hurts them hurts him, just like the teammates on a soccer or debate team, or any group that shares the work and the benefits.

CL encourages students to see peers through the cooperative window, as resources, as people to share with, as fellow adventurers in the search for knowledge. Clearly, individual work and competition still have their place, particularly when preparing students for the world outside school. With CL, we attempt to tilt the balance in favor of cooperation, not to eliminate the other two perspectives.

Furthermore, it can be argued that rarely does only one perspective apply. For instance, let's return to our tennis example above. While I may want to win, if my opponent plays much worse than I, it's not much fun, but if my opponent plays very well, I get a good challenge. Thus the person I'm playing with is both my opponent and my partner.

THE BENEFITS OF COOPERATIVE LEARNING

Research has shown that by participating in CL, students can benefit in the following areas:

- Improved academic achievement
- More active involvement in learning by students, regardless of past achievement level or individual learning needs
- Increased motivation to learn
- Increased student responsibility for their own learning
- Improved interethnic relations and acceptance of academically challenged students
- Improved time on task (sometimes dramatically improved, compared to whole-class, teacher-led instruction)
- Improved collaborative skills
- Increased liking for school
- Improved student attitudes toward learning, school, peers, and self
- Increased ability to appreciate and consider a variety of perspectives
- Greater opportunities for the teacher to observe and assess student learning

Books listed in Resources, in Part III, describe some of the research on which this list is based. If you have tried CL, no doubt you could add some benefits of your own.

A Brief Historical Note

Although we can trace the roots of cooperative learning back at least 100 years, and even thousands of years, the term *cooperative learning* seems to have arisen in the 1970s. It was at that time that an ever-expanding flow of research and practical work began to gather force. Many people have made, and continue to make, major and minor contributions to this vibrant flow. Many of the best-known of these contributors are mentioned in this book.

HOW TO GET THE MOST FROM THIS BOOK

The best way to use this book is, as you read, to try out the ideas and techniques with your students. Keep in mind that, as with any new approach, there is going to be a transitional time during which things will not go as well as you hoped. You may be tempted to give up, but please stick with it.

At the same time that you are learning a new way to teach, your students are learning a new way to learn, as well as the content you are teaching. Your class may be the exception that gets it completely the first time you try CL, but it's more common that the first three or four times are a little rough, and then, as the students start to understand why they are working in groups and become comfortable with the new classroom routines, you start to see the benefits.

If you can, find a colleague who is willing to try CL with you or who already uses CL. Having someone with whom to share your challenges, successes, and insights can be valuable. Just as a key premise of CL is that students can learn better when working with peers, so, too, can teachers. See Frequently Asked Questions in Part II for more ideas about teacher–teacher collaboration.

KEY POINTS

Aside from learning new instructional techniques, we hope you also take away from this book these two key points:

1. Cooperation among students is powerful.

   The general concept of collaboration for learning is one of the best-researched topics in all of education, with hundreds, if not thousands, of studies, over more than 100 years, from many countries, in many subject areas, and with students of a wide range of ages. These studies found that activities that support cooperation are usually associated with gains in academic, emotional, and social areas.

2. Just because students are in a group does not mean that they are cooperating.

   Students just don't get into groups and then, BOOM! start cooperating brilliantly. Indeed, sometimes working in a poorly functioning group can be worse than working alone. Group work does not equal CL. Instead, CL represents the accumulated experience of more than 100 years of trial and error, theorizing, and research on how best to help students learn together. In this book, we share some of that experience with you. No doubt, in time, you will be able to contribute innovations and variations of your own.

A NOTE ABOUT NAMES FOR TECHNIQUES

Kearney (1993) noted that attempting to attribute specific CL techniques to individuals "was like trying to catch the first drop of rain" (p. 2). Instead, Kearney attributed some techniques to those who popularized them, some to those who gave them a name that stuck, and others to those who formalized the techniques. Kearney also found that as he explained CL techniques to educators, they sometimes told him that they had developed similar techniques on their own but hadn't given them "fancy names."

Our experience has been a bit like Kearney's. Furthermore, not all the CL techniques in this book are described exactly as we found them in the original sources. In the spirit of cooperating to make CL work even more effectively, we invite other educators to use, and improvise on, our work.

ACKNOWLEDGMENTS

We gratefully acknowledge the contributions of the following reviewers:

Marguerite Terrill
    Associate Professor
    Department of Teacher Development and Professional Development
    Central Michigan University
    Mount Pleasant, MI

Audrey Skrupskelis
    Associate Professor, Elementary/Early Childhood Education
    School of Education
    University of South Carolina, Aiken
    Aiken, SC

Kelly Scrivner
    Director of Development
    St. Clement's School
    El Paso, TX

Sarah Rees Edwards
    Adjunct Professor
    University of Arizona
    Tucson, AZ

Gail Rachor
    Independent Educational Consultant
    Adjunct Professor
    Eastern Michigan University
    Ypsilanti, MI
    Adjunct Professor
    Central Michigan University
    Mount Pleasant, MI

We also wish to thank Lynda Baloche, Andy Jacobs, Joe Laturnau, and Jon Scaife for their feedback on draft versions of the book.

About the Authors

George M. Jacobs has a PhD in Educational Psychology from the University of Hawaii and a master's degree in Linguistics from the University of Illinois—Chicago. He has been teaching courses on cooperative learning since 1988. He has published many articles on the topic and is also a coauthor of *Learning Cooperative Learning via Cooperative Learning: A Sourcebook of Lesson Plans for Teacher Education* (1997). He is a member of the Executive Board of the International Association for the Study of Cooperation in Education and editor of its newsletter. He also specializes in second-language learning and helped compile an annotated bibliography of works on group activities in second-language instruction. Contact him at gmjacobs@ pacific.net.sg.

Michael A. Power has a PhD in Educational Psychology and a master's degree in English as a Second Language from the University of Hawaii. He is the Director of Instruction and Assessment for the Mercer Island, Washington, school district. He has taught English as a second language in the United States, Japan, and the Republic of Korea, and has, for many years, conducted training throughout the Pacific in instructional strategies for teachers (including cooperative learning).

Loh Wan Inn has an EdD in Science Education from the State University of New Jersey and master's degrees in Education (First Honors) and in Arts from Trinity College, University of Dublin. She is a chartered biologist (Institute of Biology, UK). She has lived and worked in the United States, Singapore, Ireland, and Australia. She has taught courses on science, mathematics, science education, environmental education, cooperative learning, curriculum design, and multiple intelligences. Through her interest in cooperative learning, she has seen it introduced in science by preschool and secondary school teachers as part of their science education modules. She also designs and trains teachers for camps on multiple intelligences and science. Her previous books include storybooks for young children and books on science and science education. She is also a member of a number of environmental organizations.

To David Sherrill and Bob Gibson, who teach by example.

Part I

Getting Started With Cooperative Learning

1

Principle: Cooperation as a Value

KEY QUESTIONS

How can I get my class started using cooperative learning (CL)?

What classroom management techniques might work well with CL?

How might the room be arranged for CL?

COOPERATIVE LEARNING TECHNIQUES INTRODUCED IN THIS CHAPTER

Find Someone Who

Two Facts, One Fiction

Classroom Classifieds

Cooperative Games

COOPERATION AS A VALUE

This chapter highlights the cooperative learning principle of Cooperation as a Value. In other words, cooperation offers not just a way of learning but also a way of life. Cooperation represents a value that we hope students will come to espouse. This does not mean that students should never compete or never work on their own. Both competition and working alone play important roles in life.

Cooperation as a Value means encouraging students to see mutual assistance as a goal to strive for, to view others as potential collaborators, and to choose cooperation as often as possible as a viable alternative to competition and individual work. Dickinson Chan (personal communication to George Jacobs, Hong Kong, October 2001), a primary school language arts teacher, put it beautifully: "The development of cooperation starts in the classroom (a small river), but students take this spirit of cooperation with them as they go out into the wide world (the ocean)."

CL is not just part of the *how* (the method) of learning; it can also be part of the *what* (the content), as cooperation is woven throughout the learning environment. For instance, students can study about how organisms cooperate with one another within and across species (Forest, 2001). Furthermore, cooperation does not stop when a CL group activity ends. To build a learning climate in which students voluntarily choose cooperation, students need opportunities to do things not just as a small group but also as a class working together toward common goals.

Some classrooms seem to be based on principles that discourage cooperation among students. Table 1.1 lists a number of the differences between such classrooms and cooperative classrooms.

What Can I Tell My Students to Get Them to Give Cooperation a Try?

Here are a few talking points for persuading students that CL is worth a go:

Research shows that students working cooperatively learn more. Thus it makes them more successful academically.

Table 1.1   Classroom Cooperation

Classrooms That Discourage Cooperation	*Cooperative Classrooms*
Eyes on your own paper.	Look at what peers are doing in order to learn from them, help them, and share ideas and materials.
No talking to your neighbor.	Talk to your neighbor in order to exchange ideas, debate, explain, suggest, and question.
Do your own work and let others do theirs.	Share your work with others so that the work you do together becomes better than the sum of its parts.
If you need help, ask the teacher.	If you need help, ask groupmates and others before asking the teacher.
Compete for the teacher's attention.	Allow each student an opportunity to be spokesperson for the group.
Compete for extrinsic rewards, e.g., grades.	Cooperate for both extrinsic and intrinsic rewards.

Learning to cooperate is important in working with others within a family, with friends and neighbors, on the job, and in life generally.

Cooperation helps students learn how to make friends and to get along with a wide variety of people.

Cooperation makes learning activities more enjoyable.

Some students respond to the honey analogy: A spirit of cooperation helps the class stick together and makes it a sweeter place to be, a place where everyone wants to be. When students like a class, they learn more.

Parents and other caretakers can also help encourage students to work cooperatively. Therefore it is often valuable to inform parents that the class will be using CL and why. This can be done via notes home or on parents' nights. Furthermore, students can get a broader perspective on the value of cooperation by asking their parents and other adults about their experiences working cooperatively in groups at school, at work, and in the community.

BUILDING A CLIMATE OF COOPERATION

Classroom atmosphere forms a key ingredient in the success of cooperative learning. For instance, students need to

- Feel comfortable working with classmates
- Be willing to share ideas, ask questions, take risks

To create such a cooperative atmosphere and to make the principle of Cooperation as a Value come alive, we can do *classbuilding activities*. *Classbuilding* means working to build a feeling of trust and solidarity among all the members of the class. Creating the right environment is crucial. Everyone has experienced how the setting we are in greatly affects what we do and how we feel.

Working with students to develop a set of behaviors, policies, or norms offers one means of promoting Cooperation as a Value. Here are some that various classes have come up with. Note the positive way they are worded, for example, "I listen when others are talking" instead of "Don't talk when others are talking." It is helpful to have these norms posted on the wall for all (including visitors) to see.

- I listen when others are talking.
- I encourage everyone to participate.
- I help others without doing the work for them.
- I ask for help when I need it.
- I am critical of ideas, not people.
- I remember that we are all in this together.

- I value and respect each person as an individual, as a groupmate, and as part of our class regardless of race, religion, nationality, or academic performance.
- I come to class on time.

We call these norms rather than rules because norms flow from shared values, such as the value of cooperation.

Class Meetings

Classroom norms are one of many possible items for the agenda of class meetings. Some teachers encourage regular class meetings to provide a safe venue for students and the teacher to air feedback—positive and negative—and suggestions on how the class is functioning. In order for students to really feel free to voice their opinions, the classroom norms listed above should also apply to class meetings.

Team Then Teacher (TTT)

TTT encourages students to see classmates as a resource rather than as competitors and helps students move away from relying exclusively on the teacher. TTT simply means that students should consult with group-mates before asking the teacher. This refers to asking about procedures as well as about content. TTT promotes group autonomy, a concept discussed in Chapter 8. Furthermore, because we want to promote classwide solidarity, students can also consult other groups before going to the teacher. Similarly, groups that finish early can offer to help others who are still working. By helping other groups, students live the principle of Cooperation as a Value.

RSPA

Teachers introducing CL often need a strategy to get students' attention when they are working in groups. For instance, teachers need to get students' attention when it is time to move to another activity or to share a good idea from one group with the rest of the class. Some teachers ring a bell; some bang on the board or switch the lights on and off. We've even heard of a high school teacher who starts to sing. Similarly, some early childhood teachers begin singing a short song and then the children sing along. When the song ends, the whole class is ready to pay attention to what the teacher wants to announce.

Different attention techniques will be right for different teachers. One commonly used signal is **RSPA**. Here is how it works. The teacher claps and raises one hand. When students hear or see these signals, they

- **R**aise a hand.
- **S**top talking.

- **P**ass the signal.
- **A**ttend to the teacher.

Pass the signal means that if students notice others who have not seen or heard the teacher's signal, they tap them on the shoulder, whisper *pssst*, or otherwise pass the signal to them.

We should discuss with students why such a signal is needed, just as we explain and involve them in other classroom decisions. Furthermore, students will enjoy using the signal themselves when they are leading the class. RSPA is an example of a class routine that helps classwide cooperation flow smoothly.

Establishing Routines

Classrooms have many routines, such as passing out papers, handing them in, or getting into groups. RSPA and signals like it are useful routines for classes using cooperative learning. Students need to spend time to understand why these routines are important and to figure out how to do them as efficiently as possible. Equally important, students can spend time *practicing* the routines. Additionally, after a period of time, such as a month, the routines may not be working as well as before. If so, we should again spend time with the class to evaluate and renew the routines. This is time well spent, because routines save precious time for learning.

Another way to promote the use of effective classroom routines is for the teacher to call the class's attention to groups that are working well together, for instance, heeding the attention signal. We point out what specific behavior the group is using. In this way, that group becomes a model for the entire class. Some teachers even time how long it takes for the class to come to attention. As an integrated mathematics activity, students can plot the times on a graph to find out if the class is making progress in functioning more smoothly.

Arranging the Classroom for Cooperative Learning

Several points need to be considered in arranging the classroom for effective collaboration. Students need to sit close together. The closer together they are, the easier it is to share materials and to use quiet voices that can't be heard by other groups. In this way, the seating arrangement fosters cooperation. Often, we can see that a group isn't functioning well just by the way a group is sitting. For example, one student is too far away from the rest of the group, or the students at either end of the group are too far away from each other to communicate easily. Figure 1.1 illustrates two kinds of seating plans.

Space needs to be provided for us to circulate around the classroom to visit all the groups. Ideally, we should have space to get between groups and the wall so that when we look up after listening to a group, we can see

Figure 1.1 Seating arrangements can foster student cooperation. Effective group seating allows all students in a group to sit close together so they can share material and use quiet voices that can't be heard by other groups.

Ineffective Group Seating

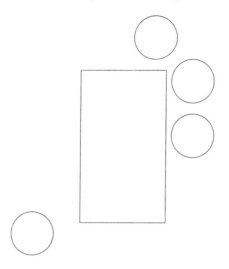

Effective Group Seating

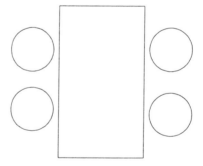

the entire class (see Figure 1.2). Also, students need room to visit other groups and to get any materials they might need. (See Part II for tips on observing students at work.)

Preferably, students should be sitting with their groupmates all the time, and they should not have to move to get into groups. However, sometimes movement will be necessary. This is another instance where routines can be useful.

For some CL activities, all students have numbers—1, 2, 3, 4. If all the students with that same number, that is, all the number 1's, are seated in the same place in their groups, such as in the southeast corner of their group, it is easier for the students and for us to know who in each group has which number.

Figure 1.2   Space needs to be provided for teachers to circulate around the entire classroom to visit all groups.

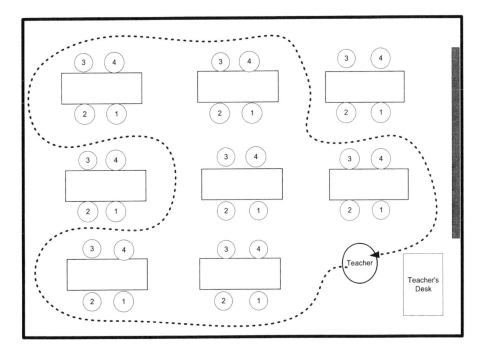

If students need to have their backs to the front of the class when working in their groups, when the class shifts to whole-class interaction, they should quietly turn their chairs to face the front of the room. Otherwise, students will feel very uncomfortable having to turn their heads 180 degrees, or they won't bother turning around and, as a result, won't be able to follow what we or others are saying or showing. Perhaps the best seating arrangement for avoiding this problem is for students to sit sideways to the front of the room, two groupmates shoulder to shoulder, facing their two other groupmates.

If furniture does need to be moved, tape on the floor or other kinds of aids can help students quickly rearrange the desks in an orderly manner when switching between group work and whole-class instruction.

In preschool, kindergarten, and younger elementary classes, students sometimes sit on the floor. In these settings, during CL, all members of the same group should either be on the floor or sitting in chairs or at desks. If some are on the floor and others at desks, it makes it difficult for us to monitor the activity, and some students have to look up to see their groupmates.

WHAT ARE SOME FUN CLASSBUILDING ACTIVITIES TO GET MY CLASS STARTED?

Find Someone Who

This activity offers a good way for students to get to know their classmates. Here is how it works.

Step 1. Students begin in pairs. Each person has a Find Someone Who table (Table 1.2 is an example). Students take turns reading the rules. Number 1 reads the first rule, number 2 paraphrases (or repeats) the rule.

Rules:

- Walk up to a classmate and ask a question from the sheet. If the person doesn't answer yes to that question, keep asking questions until they answer yes to a question.
- Have the person sign her or his name in the appropriate box. Ask the person a follow-up question and write the answer in the box.
- After someone says yes to a question, move on to another person. Each classmate should be in only one box.
- Try to fill in all the boxes.

Step 2. After about 10 minutes, students rejoin their partners and check their partner's Find Someone Who table to see if it is properly filled in and to offer suggestions about where to find people to fill in the empty boxes.

Step 3. When a couple of students have completed the table, the partners again check each other's tables.

Step 4. The teacher goes through the table, calling on students to name a person for each box. Students use their partner's sheet to respond, including their partner's follow-up question.

In designing the Find Someone Who table, teachers use their knowledge of students to make it likely that at least one student in the class will be able to write her or his name in each box and that every student will be able to say yes to at least one question. Also, some boxes can be left blank so that students can think of their own questions. Please note that space is left in each box for the person's signature and the short answer they give to the follow-up question.

Two Facts, One Fiction

This is another classbuilding activity to help students get to know each other better. It can be used at any time but is especially effective for classbuilding in the first weeks of school.

Step 1. All group members think of two things about themselves that are true (facts) and one that is not (the fiction).

Step 2. One at a time, each student tells groupmates the three self-descriptive statements without saying which is fiction and which are nonfiction. A student might say, "I have a dog. I live in an apartment. I can juggle."

Step 3. Groupmates ask questions to try to figure out which statement is fiction, such as "What kind of dog food does your dog eat?"

Step 4. Groupmates work together to guess which statement is fictitious and give reasons for their guesses.

Table 1.2   Find Someone Who . . .

Read a good book recently.	Visited a museum in the last 6 months.	Knows the formula for calculating percentage.	Has a relative or neighbor who is a teacher.
Knows a good Web site to visit.	Takes public transportation to school.	Can spell a word with more than 11 letters.	Plays volleyball.
Is a vegetarian or would like to be one someday.	Is good at growing plants.	Helped build a Web site.	Participates in recycling.
Has met a famous person.	Sent an e-mail in the last week.	Has at least one living grandparent.	Did volunteer work this year.
Prefers learning alone.	Prefers learning in groups.	Likes many kinds of music.	Walks to school.
Woke up more than 90 minutes before school.	Has a suggestion for improving our school.	Has a suggestion for improving our country.	Knows which continent Singapore is on.
Knows the stages in a butterfly's life cycle.	Can play a musical instrument.	Has participated in a band, chorus, or other musical group.	Can stand on her or his shoulders or head.
Is thinking of becoming a teacher.	Likes to eat sandwiches made of weird combinations.	Slept 10 hours or more last Sunday.	Can juggle.

Step 5. Groupmates share with the class something interesting they learned about each of their group members.

The teacher should get the ball rolling by modeling the process. For example, a teacher uses these three self-descriptive statements: "I was on my high school tennis team. I was on my high school debate team. I was on my high school wrestling team."

This activity is a good way for students to learn about their classmates and to develop a sense of trust by revealing things about themselves. Two Facts, One Fiction, as well as Find Someone Who, can be used not just for classbuilding but also to teach content. For instance, instead of students coming up with three statements about themselves, their statements can relate to topics the class is studying.

Two Facts, One Fiction can be called Two Truths, One Exaggeration or, for younger children, Yes, Yes, No.

Classroom Classifieds (Sapon-Shevin, 1999)

In Classroom Classifieds, students write short classified advertisements with things that they can teach or help with, or things they want to learn or need some help on. Examples of areas in which students can help one another are making origami, becoming better organized, finding a partner for chess, getting along with parents, and learning a new language. This activity can be an ongoing one, continuing throughout the year.

A related idea from Sapon-Shevin's (1999) inspiring book is Classroom Yellow Pages, in which students list what they can teach or share. By helping classmates and receiving help from classmates, students build stronger ties. Also, students who may be weaker than average academically get a chance to be the helper instead of always being the one receiving help.

Cooperative Games

Everyone enjoys playing games, but many games stress competition over cooperation. At the end of competitive games, one person or one team is the winner, and everyone else is a loser. In contrast, cooperative games combine the fun of games with the principle of Cooperation as a Value. Some of these cooperative games are traditional games, others are modifications of competitive games, and still others are newly invented. Three books (Grineski, 1996; Orlick, 1978, 1981) that describe cooperative games are included in the Resources section of this book.

One example of a cooperative game that was created by modifying a competitive game is Cooperative Musical Chairs (Luvmour & Luvmour, 1990, p. 27). In competitive Musical Chairs, one by one the chairs are removed, and with each chair removed, out goes another player. However, with Cooperative Musical Chairs, the goal is inclusion, not exclusion.

When the music stops, everyone must find a way to share chairs so that everyone stays in the game. Players can share seats, link arms, or use whatever device they can think of to keep everyone playing. Creative problem solving comes in handy here. Cooperative Musical Chairs wouldn't be appropriate for all students, but we can find ways to transform almost any game from competitive to cooperative.

Marc Hegelsen (personal communication, December 18, 2001, e-mail from Japan) suggests another way of keeping everyone in Musical Chairs. Whoever is *it* (the one left without a chair when the music stops) contributes an idea to the group. The idea could be on a topic the group is discussing, a task the group is doing, a story the group is composing, or just something about the person who is *it*.

COMING ATTRACTIONS

This first chapter offered ideas on how to foster a cooperative spirit among students. This spirit provides an important groundwork for the principle to be discussed in Chapter 2, Heterogeneous Grouping. This principle concerns the formation of small groups of students that are representative of the different types of students found in the class.

2

Principle: Heterogeneous Grouping

KEY QUESTIONS

How can I form cooperative groups?

How can I help my students work together smoothly?

What are some strategies for teambuilding?

COOPERATIVE LEARNING TECHNIQUES INTRODUCED IN THIS CHAPTER

Team Mascots

Circle of Interviewers

Forward Snowball

Reverse Snowball

Physical Education Teambuilding Game

HETEROGENEOUS GROUPING

In Chapter 1, we discussed the principle of Cooperation as a Value. Chapter 2 discusses the principle of Heterogeneous Grouping. The idea is that students should cooperate with a wide range of people, not just those with whom they want to cooperate. Thus in cooperative learning, although students may occasionally work in groups of their own choice, they most often work in teacher-assigned, heterogeneous groups.

Reasons for Heterogeneous Grouping

Although it's taking the path of least resistance to let students work with their friends, there are a number of good reasons for heterogeneous groups:

- Students get to know people different from themselves through working toward a common goal.
- The quality of student work can improve because of the mixture of different perspectives.
- The more diligent students can provide positive role models.
- Discipline may improve, because students may be more likely to misbehave if they are with their friends.
- The diversity of ideas can increase.
- Students may develop skills to work with people different from themselves, especially those with whom they would not have chosen to collaborate. These skills are useful beyond school, as we don't often get to choose with whom we work or share a neighborhood.
- More helping may occur as higher achievers assist lower achievers.

Criteria for Forming Heterogeneous Groups

Here are some things we will want to consider when creating groups that will represent a cross section of the skills and characteristics present in our class:

- Achievement level
- Aptitude level
- Work attitude
- Ethnicity
- Personality (e.g., extrovert or introvert)
- Social class
- Gender
- Special needs

If we use heterogeneous groups of four, we also need to pay attention to the composition of pairs when we divide fours into twos.

Other Grouping Options

While teacher-selected, heterogeneous groups are most common in CL classrooms, other group formation techniques might be considered for occasional use:

- Students form groups with whomever is sitting near them. (This is the quickest way to form groups.)
- Groups form randomly. For instance, if we have a class of 24 and want groups of four, the class can count off to six. Then, all the 1's form a group, all the 2's, and so forth.
- Students decide on their partners. Students often prefer this option, sometimes rather strongly.
- Groups form based on commonalities, for example, common interests, as is sometimes done in Group Investigation (see Chapter 8).
- Groups form based on student selection of tasks. For example, if (in a class of 24) we offer the students a choice of one of six tasks, then groups can consist of either all students who chose the same task, or students can form groups so that all tasks are represented in each group.
- Homogeneous groups do short-term tasks. For instance, the high achievers collaborate on an enrichment task, and low achievers help each other to try again on some material that they did not master the first time through.

STUDENT REACTION TO HETEROGENEOUS GROUPS

One goal behind the use of heterogeneous grouping is not just that students learn to collaborate with groupmates of all kinds but that they come to appreciate the benefits of diversity and come to *want* to work in mixed groups, not just grudgingly accept it.

Also, we should explain to students what heterogeneous grouping means, the benefits of heterogeneous groups, and the various ways to make groups. Some talking points for this discussion, in addition to the ones cited earlier in this chapter, are as follows:

- As adults, we are often thrown together with different kinds of people. In addition to colleagues, we also have to interact with a wide variety of patients, customers, suppliers, and others. Students prepare themselves for this by working in diverse groups at school.
- Countries, in most cases, are increasingly heterogeneous. We need to learn how to deal with this diversity and, hopefully, appreciate the benefits that diversity brings. This connects to the CL principle of Cooperation as a Value (Chapter 1).
- We live in an increasingly global world. For instance, the Internet and e-mail put us instantly in touch with people all over the world. By learning to get along with people different from ourselves, we put ourselves in a better position to enjoy citizenship in our more diverse world.
- Some high-achieving students may complain about being asked to help their lower-achieving classmates. They feel that as a result,

they miss the opportunity to work at a level they find challenging. Some points that address this concern include the following:

– Students learn a topic best by teaching others. As the saying goes, "Those who teach learn twice."
– In many professions that high achievers aspire to, such as medicine, management, and law, the ability to teach others is crucial. For example, doctors teach patients how to look after their own health.
– It is important that no student get typecast in any one role. The use of different roles and multiple-ability tasks (Chapter 6) is one way to address this.
– Students with high aptitude need time to work at their own level (alone and in groups with others at their level) in addition to time working with classmates at different levels.

Based on the discussion of heterogeneity, we can get student input on group formation. One community college teacher we know first tells students about the benefits of heterogeneous groups. Then he lets students form their own groups as long as they meet his heterogeneity criteria.

One Teacher's Experience

Despite the reasons for using teacher-selected, heterogeneous groups, it's common for teachers to allow students to choose groups based on friendship. However, this has inherent problems, as shown in the experience of one teacher we know who started the year allowing students to choose their own groupmates and found that the class was too cliquish:

To get around the cliques, at the beginning of the second semester, I made an attempt to bring about a more cohesive homeroom class by changing the seating plan. I had allowed the students to sit with their close buddies during the first semester, and I found unity was lacking in the class. To improve the situation, I arranged to have a male student seated next to a female, in pairs. Also, as the class is multiracial, a student is seated next to one of a different race.

As I expected, a few students were quite resentful at first, and some of them hardly spoke to their new partners. However, as I've been using more CL, gaps have been bridged, and social integration is taking place. In CL activities, the students have no choice but to work with the ones sitting next to them, some of whom they would never speak to otherwise.

How Big Should CL Groups Be?

In this book, you will notice that most of the CL techniques involve pairs or foursomes, or foursomes divided into pairs. Groups of four have many advantages in terms of both management and learning:

- Groups larger than four become more difficult for students to manage.
- Fours divide into pairs, for the greatest amount of student interaction, and then can quickly reform into foursomes.
- The larger the group, the easier it is for one person to hide or be neglected.
- Pairs can talk together and then, rather than reporting to the whole class, they can report to the other pair in their foursome.
- Fours have an advantage over pairs because having two more members can mean more ideas and more people power to carry out tasks.

Other factors can affect the choice a teacher makes regarding optimum group size. For instance, equipment can be a factor: If there are only six microscopes for 30 students, then groups of five may be best. Larger groups mean fewer groups for us to supervise, and if each group produces one product, we have fewer products to evaluate.

How big is too big? The maximum size of groups depends on many factors, but we have found that groups larger than six lead to difficulties for three reasons:

- There is a greater tendency for some students to do more than their share of the work.
- Students may lack the skills to coordinate a larger group.
- Students may form smaller groups with their friends within the group.

Younger children, especially, may need smaller groups. Remember also, please, that a pair is also a group. Indeed, as stated above, most of the activities in this book are done in groups of four or two.

Actually Forming the Groups

One way to divide a class into heterogeneous groups is to take a class roster and put students in order based on the factor that is most important to distribute among groups, for example, past achievement. Then we put the highest, the lowest, and the two middle achievers in the same group. The second group is composed of the second-highest, second-lowest, two more from the middle, and so on. Next, we look at how we've done in terms of the factor we feel is second most important to distribute, for example, ethnicity: If the highest, lowest, and two middle achievers are all Hispanic, we need to do a bit of changing around.

Table 2.1 shows one way to create mixed groups of students so that each group includes a mixture for whichever criteria we select, such as achievement or motivation.

Cohen (1994) suggests that the most efficient way to compose and recompose groups over the year is to make or buy a chart that has pockets for cards representing class members (available from many teacher supply houses).

Table 2.1   Chart Showing How Students Can Be Put Into Six Groups of Four

Student Rank on the Selected Criterion	Group Number					
	1	2	3	4	5	6
1	X					
2		X				
3			X			
4				X		
5					X	
6						X
7						X
8					X	
9				X		
10			X			
11		X				
12	X					
13	X					
14		X				
15			X			
16				X		
17					X	
18						X
19						X
20					X	
21				X		
22			X			
23		X				
24	X					

Other Points to Consider

One point to keep in mind in doing all this sorting is that for some factors, such as gender, we probably don't want to have only one of a kind in a group, for example, one male and three females. One alternative lies in having even numbers of females and males for as many groups as possible. If we run out of one gender, all four members of the rest of the groups are the same sex. For instance, in a class of 32 with 18 females and 14 males, we have seven groups of two females and two males (total of 28) and one all-female group (total of four).

Another issue that arises in forming groups is what to do with students who, for whatever reason (e.g., hyperactivity or because they are bullied), are isolated from their classmates. Other students may not want these students in their groups, and groups may have difficulty functioning with students who have serious problems relating to others. What we can do here is identify students in the class who have the skills for dealing with such students, speak with them privately to ask their help, give them some pointers, and then monitor the groups carefully. Students who speak English as a second language and need help with the language can be put in a group with a classmate who speaks their first language and is better with English.

Finally, some CL experts, such as Cohen (1994), warn against forming heterogeneous groups in a transparent way; for example, in a class with two ethnic groups, all groups have two members of one ethnic group and two of the other. Cohen fears that this might lead students to see groupmates of the other ethnicity not as people but as representatives of that ethnicity. On the other hand, if we are upfront with students about how we decided on forming groups and the reasons for our decision, and if we do teambuilding activities (as described later in this chapter), the problem may diminish.

How Often Should I Change the Groups?

Doing all the work involved in dividing the class into heterogeneous groups and then building trust and solidarity in the groups leads to a temptation to keep the same groups for an entire year. Students may also prefer this as they get comfortable working in the same group. Nonetheless, it is a good idea to change groups regularly. We prefer to change groups about four times a year for the following reasons:

- Students learn to work with a wide range of partners, each with varied skills and experiences.
- Students have an opportunity to learn how to work with new partners; cliques are less likely to form.
- Students realize that the whole class, not just the one group they currently belong to, benefits from cooperation.
- Resistance to heterogeneous grouping is lessened, because students don't have to spend the entire year in a group with the same groupmates.

Before changing groups, we like to have a closing activity. For example, students write their groupmates thank-you notes or letters of reference to take to their next group.

WHY DO TEAMBUILDING?

Slavin (1995) points out that when we use teacher-selected heterogeneous grouping, the resulting combination of students is likely to be one that would never have been created had it not been for our intervention. Thus when students get into new groups, they need time to develop trust and solidarity within their group. Teambuilding activities can help with this. Many such activities can be found in books of cooperative games and outdoor activities.

Why spend valuable class time on nonacademic matters? Because a feeling of safety and belonging enhances learning. One way to facilitate this feeling is the use of low-risk teambuilding activities that everyone feels comfortable doing. For example, not everyone feels comfortable singing and dancing, so we wouldn't want to do teambuilding activities that involve solo singing or dancing. Indeed, our initial CL activities should attempt to play to success so that students feel they can collaborate effectively.

Being a member of a group provides students with a feeling of inclusion. This can be particularly important for students who are different from the mainstream. Psychologists Deci and Ryan (1985) suggest that human beings have three universal needs—relatedness, competence, and autonomy. CL helps to meet all three needs.

Let's begin with relatedness. Relatedness refers to being connected to others. In a CL classroom, we move away from an eyes-on-your-own paper, no-talking-to-your-neighbor style of teaching that separates pupils from one another. The point is that students can focus better on their studies when they feel connected to those around them. (In upcoming chapters, we will discuss Deci and Ryan's two other universal needs, competence and autonomy.) Last but not least, we can combine teambuilding with academic content, for example, when using the CL technique Forward Snowball, described later in this chapter.

HOW TO DO TEAMBUILDING

We have many ways to help students build strong teams. For instance, we should not object if groups spend a bit of time chitchatting. After all, this chitchat offers a way of creating a relaxed, trusting atmosphere in the group. Furthermore, a key reason for using heterogeneous groups is to allow students from diverse backgrounds to get to know each other as people, rather than as members of a particular ethnic group, gender, and so forth.

Here are some simple teambuilding activities. Note that while some of these activities are designed to be used when groups first form, an occasional short teambuilding activity may be useful any time team solidarity seems to need a bit of a boost.

Team Mascots

1. Each student in a group has a half sheet of paper.

2. Near the top of the paper, they draw a pair of eyes, being as imaginative as they wish.

3. Students pass the paper to their left and draw a nose to fit the eyes on the paper they have received.

4. They pass again and draw a mouth to match the eyes and nose, and pass again, and draw ears.

5. The papers return to the students who started them. They add whatever they wish to the drawings—a body, hair, nose rings.

6. The group looks at all the drawings and chooses one as their mascot. They name their mascot. The name can relate to the subject of the course (e.g., Algie, the Algebra Gorilla).

Rationale: Creating their mascot, as a team, gives group members something in common, something that they all had a part in creating. A variation on Team Mascots is Team Logo, in which the students cooperate to design and illustrate a logo that will identify their group and that somehow represents the characteristics or contributions of the members.

Circle of Interviewers

This CL technique (see Figure 2.1) is good for teambuilding and many other purposes as well. Each student in a foursome has a number: 1, 2, 3, or 4.

Step 1. Student 1 interviews student 2. At the same time, student 3 interviews student 4.

Step 2. Roles are reversed. Student 2 interviews student 1, and student 4 interviews student 3.

Step 3. The interviewers take a turn to report what they learned in their interview.

Step 4. If time permits, group members ask each other follow-up questions.

Here are two teambuilding games from Sapon-Shevin (1999) that have been adapted for use with Circle of Interviewers.

Little-Known Facts About Me

Students write one or two things about themselves that their groupmates do not know, such as, "I have a relative who lives in another country," or "My ideal career is to be a talk show host." Then students do Circle of Interviewers, asking, "What is something that you think the rest of us in this group do not know about you?" The interviewers ask at least one follow-up question.

Lifelines

Each student draws a straight line. At one end of the line is the year they were born; at the other end is the current year. Students mark and label six to ten points along the line with significant events in their lives, such as the year their family adopted another child, when they moved to a new place, or when the student started playing soccer. This is their lifeline. Then, students do Circle of Interviewers, asking questions about each other's lifelines.

Both these games help students learn about each other. As groupmates show interest in each other's lives and react positively to the information that peers disclose about themselves, a feeling of trust grows.

Other Times to Use Circle of Interviewers

Like all CL techniques, Circle of Interviewers can be used with any topic, in any subject area, and at various points in a lesson. For instance,

Figure 2.1 Circle of Interviewers is a good CL technique for teambuilding. In step 1, student 1 interviews student 2, and student 4 interviews student 3. In step 2, interviewer–interviewee roles are reversed. In step 3, individual interviewers take a turn reporting what they learned about their interviewee while the other students listen.

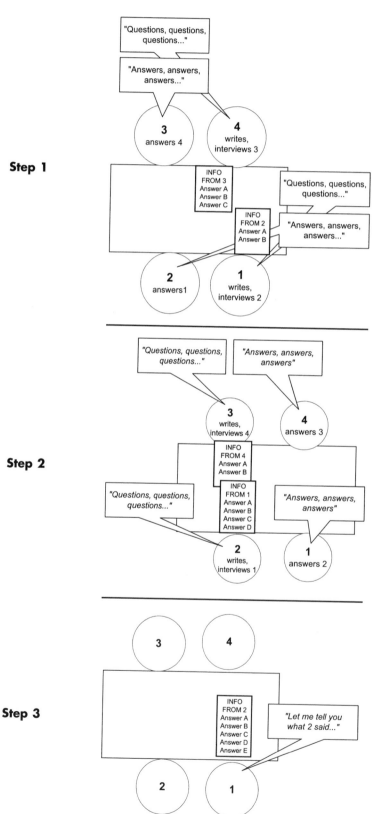

we can use it at the beginning of a lesson for pupils to discuss what they already know about the topic of the lesson or what they recall from the last lesson. Alternatively, students can do Circle of Interviewers near the end of a lesson to discuss what they learned, what wasn't clear, and what they want to know more about. Examples:

Language Arts. To accompany extensive reading, students interview each other about the books they have read.

Science. Students interview each other to find out what they know about plants and their experience with plants.

Mathematics. Students interview each other about how they would approach a particular problem. To encourage variety, students can interview their partners about a different problem, but each problem is of the same general type.

Social Studies. Students do interviews about partners' opinions on a particular policy, event, or historical figure.

Circle of Interviewers works best when interview questions are likely to produce different answers. For instance, unless students have very fertile imaginations, it wouldn't be very interesting to use "What is two times two?" as an interview question.

Forward Snowball (Kearney, 1993)

This CL technique (see Figure 2.2) highlights the benefit of heterogeneity because it is good for gathering as many ideas or as much information as possible.

Step 1. Each group member works alone to list ideas or information.

Step 2. Pairs explain their lists to each other and then make a combined list. Duplications are eliminated.

Step 3. Pair one and pair two get together and make a combined list. Duplications are eliminated.

Forward Snowball is great for teambuilding because it provides dramatic proof that two (or more) heads really are better than one.

Uses for Forward Snowball

Language Arts. The teacher writes a fairly long word on the board, such as *important.* Students do Forward Snowball to see how many words they can generate using the letters of *important.*

Mathematics. The teacher challenges students to use unconventional means to measure the girth of a tree trunk. Students use Forward Snowball to suggest the different ways of measuring, such as the use of pipe cleaners and hand spans.

Figure 2.2 Forward Snowball is a good CL technique for gathering lots of information. In step 1, each student works alone to create a list. In step 2, individual students form pairs to combine lists and eliminate duplications. In step 3, pairs of students get together, and the group creates a comprehensive, consolidated list of all relevant items.

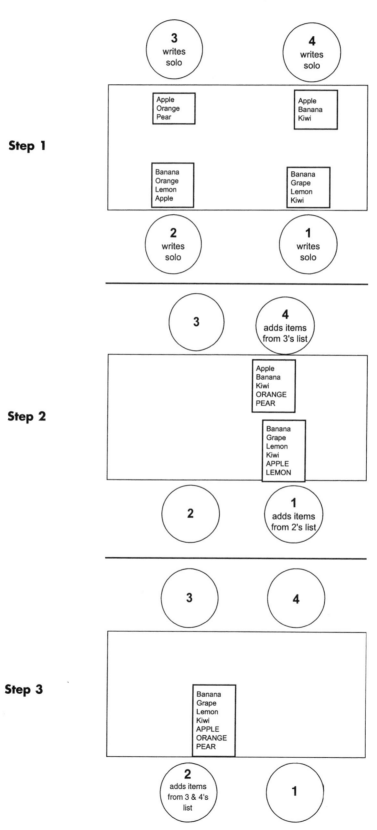

Science. The teacher writes a discussion question on the board, such as, "What are some ways that organisms ensure their own survival?" Students do Forward Snowball to list various survival techniques, such as swallowtail butterflies mimicking monarch butterflies, lizards changing colors to camouflage themselves, and wind-pollinated plants producing copious amounts of pollen.

Social Studies. The class has read about past and recent examples of discrimination. In groups, they use Forward Snowball to generate ways that the victims of discrimination and witnesses to discrimination can work against it.

Reverse Snowball (Kearney, 1993)

In Forward Snowball, the group's list gets bigger and bigger. In Reverse Snowball (Figure 2.3), it gets smaller.

Step 1. Each group member works alone to list ideas or information.

Step 2. Pairs explain their lists to each other and then make a list of only those items that appear on both lists or only those that they think are the best.

Step 3. Two pairs repeat the same process.

The Same Game

The Same Game is a teambuilding game we learned from Nanyang Technological University professor Christine Lee that has been adapted for use with Reverse Snowball.

Step 1. Each person lists a total of 12 likes or dislikes.

Step 2. Pairs explain their lists to each other and then make a list of eight common likes or dislikes. They can add ones that were not on either person's list.

Step 3. Two pairs repeat the same process, trying to come up with a list of four common likes or dislikes.

Rationale: By identifying commonalities, students come to recognize that they are not so different from their groupmates.

Uses for Reverse Snowball

Language Arts. Each group member lists four examples of good writing in a particular text. By step 3 of Reverse Snowball, they try to agree on the best example of good writing in the text.

Mathematics. Each group member lists the ways that the given data could be represented (e.g., raw data, paragraph summary, pie chart, line graph, and bar graph). Using Reverse Snowball, they try to agree on the best way to represent the particular data for a particular audience.

Figure 2.3 Reverse Snowball is a technique to use when a short list is the goal. In step 1, each student works alone to create a list. In step 2, individual students form pairs to select only the items common to both lists or the best items from the two lists. In step 3, the entire group creates a single list containing only the common items or the best items from all lists.

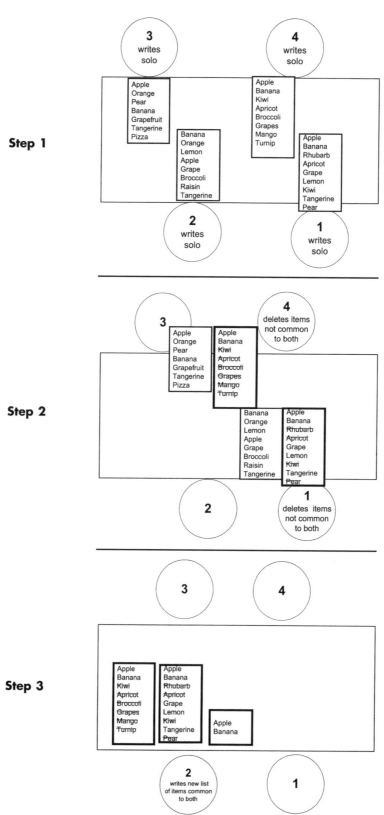

Science. Individual group members list the food that they would like to eat for dinner. Using Reverse Snowball, they eliminate foods that are unhealthy or unappealing and agree on a menu of healthy, appealing food.

Social Studies. The class has read about past and recent examples of discrimination. After they generate ways that the victims of discrimination and witnesses to discrimination can work against it, they think of situations in which they experience or witness discrimination and choose one or two ways they will use to contest the discrimination.

Physical Education Teambuilding Game

Many teambuilding activities have been developed by teachers of Physical Education (PE) and outdoor education. One of them is called Hula Hoops. Recently, one of the authors observed a PE teacher working with a new class on the first day of school. Students formed circles of six, each with a large hula hoop. The students had to link hands and, by stepping through the hoop one by one, move the hoop all the way around the circle.

At the start, the hoop was around one student's arm. He had to put his head, and then the rest of his body, through it and shift it to his neighbor on the right, all without letting go of his neighbors' hands. In addition to passing the hoop and trying to get it all the way around without breaking the circle, each student had to call out her or his name while passing the hoop.

Rationale: This activity clearly formed a strong bond within the groups as they worked together to complete a difficult task. (It's even difficult to describe!) In addition, they learned each other's names and learned that PE can be both challenging and fun. They were off to a very good start of the year.

WHAT HAPPENS AFTER TEAMBUILDING?

Now that we've done teambuilding, and students are in teams, what's next?

In addition to engaging in teambuilding and developing a classroom environment that promotes cooperation, creating a sense of common purposes ranks at the top of the list of factors that promote cohesive groups. Groups need common goals. Means of promoting united groups are discussed in the next chapter, which focuses on the principle of Positive Interdependence.

3

Principle: Positive Interdependence

KEY QUESTIONS

What is positive interdependence?

How can I help my students develop positive interdependence?

How can we encourage a "one for all, all for one" spirit among students?

COOPERATIVE LEARNING TECHNIQUES INTRODUCED IN THIS CHAPTER

Jigsaw

Jigsaw II

Student Teams Achievement Divisions (STAD)

Think–Pair–Share

Write–Pair–Switch

POSITIVE INTERDEPENDENCE

The principle of Positive Interdependence is the most important principle in cooperative learning (CL). Positive interdependence represents a feeling among group members that what helps one group member benefits all the members, and what hurts one member hurts them all. The motto of *The Three Musketeers* (Dumas, 1998) captures it best: "All for one and one for all." Paraphrasing Kagan (1998), to consider whether a group activity promotes positive interdependence, we should ask these two questions:

Is a benefit for one group member a benefit for another?

Is collaboration needed (one person alone isn't sufficient)?

If the answer to both these questions is yes, then the learning environment is helping students build positive interdependence. Let's look at some CL techniques that build positive interdependence in the context of academic lessons.

JIGSAW

Jigsaw (see Figure 3.1) is a well-known CL technique with many variations. Here we describe the basic version.

Step 1.   Students' original groups of four are called *home teams*. Each home team member receives different information. This is their piece of the jigsaw puzzle. For instance, one member might have information on the habitat of frogs, another on the anatomy of frogs, a third on the feeding and reproductive habits of frogs, and the fourth on threats to the survival of frogs.

Step 2.   Students leave their home teams and form *expert teams* composed of people from other groups who have the same piece of information. The role of the expert teams is to understand their piece and prepare to teach it to their home team members.

Step 3.   Students return to their home teams and take turns teaching their piece. Groupmates ask questions and discuss.

Step 4.   Students take an individual quiz based on information from all four pieces or work together to do a task that requires knowledge taught by all four home team members. Groups receive a nongrade reward based on their members' scores on the quiz or the quality of their task performance. (See section on STAD later in this chapter for details on this system.)

Analyzing Jigsaw

Now let's go back to the two questions about positive interdependence.

Is a benefit for one group member a benefit for another?

Yes, because by helping groupmates to understand each piece of the jigsaw, each student helps the whole group do better on the quiz or complete a better project.

Is collaboration needed (one person alone isn't sufficient)?

Yes, collaboration is needed because each student has only one piece of the text. Students depend on their groupmates to tell them about the other pieces. Thus the task cannot be done alone.

We need to encourage students to see that they do indeed depend on each other. Positive interdependence exists not primarily in the way we structure a task but primarily in the minds of students. Part of our job as teachers is to encourage students to feel that how well they work together will determine whether they sink or swim.

Pointers on Using Jigsaw

Here are a few pointers to keep in mind when using Jigsaw (for more pointers, see the Jigsaw Web site listed in Resources):

- We usually have two or more expert teams for each piece, rather than putting all the students with the same piece into one expert team. For instance, if we have 28 students, and we have four Jigsaw pieces, we would have seven students in each expert team. That's too many. So, we form two expert teams for each piece.
- All the pieces of text should be understandable on their own. For instance, if we divide a short story into four parts, the students who receive the last part may have a good deal of difficulty understanding it. What we can use in such instances is Jigsaw II (explained below) in which all students receive the entire text and then go to expert teams for close study of one piece.
- Students may need some help in knowing what to present to their home teams. We can help by giving a set of questions to the expert teams.
- Students may not be very skilful in presenting to their home teams. They may need assistance in such form as outlines or graphic organizers (e.g., word webs or mind maps). Also, students might want to rehearse their presentations in the expert team.
- To encourage home team members to pay careful attention when each of their experts is reporting, experts can quiz home team members to check their understanding of what was presented.
- Rather than teachers providing the material for Jigsaw, expert teams can begin with topics and research them on their own before reporting to their home teams.

JIGSAW II

Jigsaw II is a variation on Jigsaw. In Jigsaw, each expert is the only member of their home team with a particular piece. In Jigsaw II, everyone has all the pieces but becomes an expert on one designated piece. The advantages of Jigsaw II are that sometimes individual pieces are easier to understand after reading the entire text, and if one home team member is

Figure 3.1 In Jigsaw step 1, each home team member receives a different piece of the jigsaw puzzle. In step 2, students leave their home teams to form small expert teams with members of other home teams who have the same text piece. In step 3, students return and teach their home teams what they learned in their expert teams. In step 4, students take an individual quiz based on information in all four pieces. Alternatively, home teams can do a task that requires information from all four pieces.

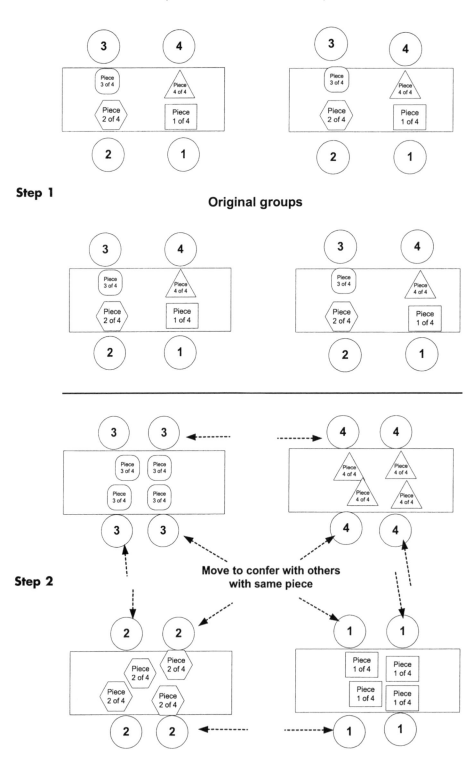

Step 1

Original groups

Step 2

Move to confer with others with same piece

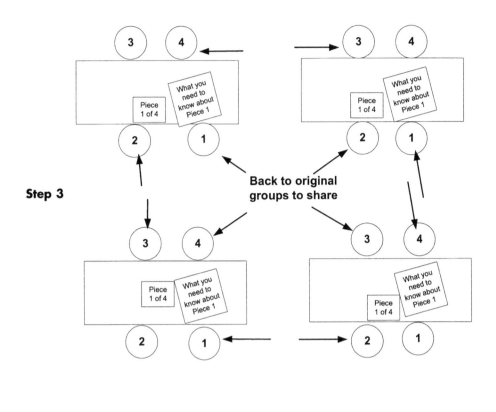

Step 3

Back to original groups to share

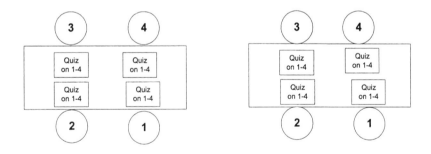

Step 4

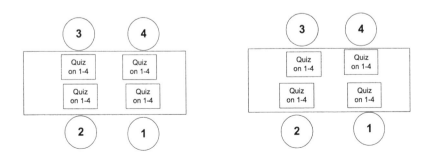

absent or does not do a good job, the team isn't stranded. On the other hand, Jigsaw II might mean a reduced feeling of positive interdependence. Many teachers find Jigsaw II easier to use, because textbooks and other readily available materials can be used without any adaptation.

One Teacher's Experience

This is what one middle school English teacher we know wrote after her class used Jigsaw:

> It was a very successful lesson because the expert teams worked very hard to be experts in their given piece. When the weaker ones had some difficulty understanding the paragraph, they asked for help, and the other experts helped them to summarize the key points in the paragraph. The slower learners got very excited and repeated their points several times to make sure that they wouldn't convey the wrong message to their home teams. Overall, I was happy that they realized individual accountability [discussed in Chapter 4] is a very important element of cooperative learning in that all students took the trouble to understand their own pieces.

Additional Types of Positive Interdependence Found in Jigsaw

Goal Positive Interdependence

Jigsaw highlights three types of positive interdependence. The first is goal positive interdependence. This simply means that the group members see themselves as sharing a common goal or goals. In Jigsaw, that goal is to learn their pieces in order to share the information with groupmates so that the group can do their task well or each member can do well on the quiz. The group's goal normally relates to the learning objectives of the lesson.

One simple way that Johnson and Johnson (1998) recommend for groups to signal that they have achieved their goal is for all members to sign their names to the group's product, to their groupmates' work, or to a statement about the lesson objectives. By signing, students are saying that they have done their share of the work, they have reviewed what their group has done, they have understood the key ideas in the lesson and learned the key skills, and all their groupmates have done the same. We can help build the feeling of goal positive interdependence by helping students to understand clearly the goals their group needs to achieve and how they need to cooperate to achieve them.

Resource Positive Interdependence

A second type of positive interdependence highlighted in Jigsaw is resource positive interdependence. Resource positive interdependence means that each group member has unique resources that they must share in order for the group to succeed. These resources can be of two types: information or material.

Information resources are the type we see in Jigsaw. Each group member has unique information and must share that information for the group to succeed. The teacher or the course materials can provide this information *to* the students. Information can also be provided *by* the students, either from knowledge they already have, such as that gained when students interview each other about their attitudes toward frogs, or from information they obtain by doing research.

The other type of resource is materials. For instance:

- In doing an experiment in science class, different group members might have different pieces of apparatus needed to conduct the experiment.
- When making a graphic organizer, each student can use a different color marker, with the goal of having all colors represented in the graphic organizer.
- Only one set of questions (or other data) can be given to the group. This paper can circulate among the members after each question.

Celebration/Reward Positive Interdependence

A third type of positive interdependence that Jigsaw encourages is celebration/reward positive interdependence. The reward that individual students receive, such as grades, praise, or stickers, depends on the rewards their groupmates receive. The use of extrinsic rewards is one of the more controversial issues in CL and in education generally. We will discuss this in more detail in Chapter 9. At this point, let us just say that while extrinsic rewards may seem useful in a particular context, or may even be required, you might want to look for ways gradually to move away from them. Or, as Baloche (1998) recommends to the preservice teachers she works with, never begin an extrinsic reward program without having a plan for how to end it.

More Variations on Positive Interdependence

In addition to goal, resource, and celebration/reward positive interdependence, there are several other types, which we will now discuss. With *role positive interdependence*, each group member has a unique role to play to help the group achieve its goals. These roles can rotate. In Chapter 6, we talk about roles that are part of role positive interdependence.

Another type of positive interdependence is *identity positive interdependence.* The idea involves helping the group to feel a common identity. Sport teams, clubs, and many other kinds of groups, even gangs, attempt to build a shared identity among members using techniques such as songs, flags, colors, cheers, and special handshakes. In Chapter 2, we looked at teambuilding—which is one way to foster identity positive interdependence.

Identity positive interdependence can work with celebration/reward positive interdependence. For instance, after successful completion of a task, a group can do their group cheer. The Success for All program (see

Table 3.1   Some Types of Positive Interdependence With Examples

Type of Positive Interdependence	Examples
Goal	Complete task specifications; improve on group's average on past quizzes.
Resource	Each group member has different information about the history of computers; each group member has a different piece of apparatus.
Celebration/Reward	If they reach their goal, the group does their team cheer or receives bonus points.
Role	One group member is facilitator, another is questioner, another is checker, and the fourth is recorder.
Identity	The group has a motto and a group handshake.
External Challenge	The group tries to reduce the amount of waste created in the school cafeteria; the group tries to create an advertisement better than one they saw on TV.

Resources) has developed many fun cheers, such as the clam clap and the accordion clap. There is no end to the various cheers groups can invent to celebrate their successes. Please note that group cheers, such as clam claps and accordion claps, can be energetic yet quiet. Another idea for promoting identity positive interdependence is for the group to have their own plant or classroom pet, for which they are responsible.

One more type of positive interdependence is *external-challenge positive interdependence*. This can sometimes involve groups competing against other groups. When we think about our larger goal of spreading the spirit of cooperation outside the small group to the entire class and beyond, we will probably want to use such intergroup competition sparingly. Fortunately, external challenges do not have to be against people. Students can compete against a standard. Just as a relay team works hard to beat their own best time, so, too, can a group or class study hard to beat their previous score or to develop ideas to overcome a problem. Table 3.1 provides a summary of the types of positive interdependence discussed in this chapter.

STUDENT TEAMS ACHIEVEMENT DIVISIONS (STAD)

One widely used CL technique that employs celebration/reward positive interdependence is STAD. The first 3 steps in this 4-step technique are simple; the last is a bit tricky:

1. The teacher provides the class with instruction on a particular topic.

2. Students study the topic further in their groups in preparation for a quiz.

3. Students take the quiz independently of their groupmates.

Table 3.2   Example of a STAD Team Point System

Points to Team	Score on Recent Quiz	Examples
30	Perfect paper (no matter what the past average is)	Su Kim gets 30 points for her team because she got a perfect score of 100, even though her past average was 97.
30	More than 10 points above past average	Bruce got 30 points for his team because he scored 89 on the quiz, which is 11 points above his past average of 78.
20	Past average to 10 points above past average	Aisha got 20 points for her team because she scored 92, and her past average was 88.
10	1 to 10 points below past average	Octavio got 10 points for his team because his score of 82 on the quiz was 3 points below his past average of 85.
0	More than 10 points below past average	Sarah did not get any points for her team because her 82 was 17 points below her past average of 98.

4. The teacher scores the quiz or students do. Now comes the tricky part (but made easier nowadays by computers). Students' scores are compared to their past average. Points are computed based on how well individual students did relative to their previous work. Table 3.2 provides an example of a STAD team point system.

Once we calculate the number of points individual students have earned for their team, these points are averaged to determine if the team will receive recognition in such forms as certificates, bulletin board notices, or the chance to do a team's handshake or silent cheer. Here, recommended by the people at Success for All (see Resources), is the STAD team recognition system based on average improvement points:

25-or-more-point average: Super Team

20-point average: Great Team

15-point average: Good Team

Ideas to Remember About STAD

One potential confusion in STAD is that STAD separates grades from contribution to the team. In the example (Table 3.2), Bruce got 30 points for his team, and Aisha got only 20 points for her team. However, Aisha's score in the grade book, 92, is higher than Bruce's 89. Thus grades are separate from nongrade team rewards, such as recognition.

Equal opportunity for success is a powerful characteristic of STAD. Equal opportunity for success means that individual group members, regardless of past achievement, have an equal opportunity to contribute to their group. This is because improvement scoring is used. So if my past average is only 25 out of 100, just by improving to 40 (more than 10 points above past average) on the next quiz, I can contribute 30 points to my

Figure 3.2 Think–Pair–Share is one the best-known CL techniques. In step 1, each student thinks about a question asked by the teacher. In step 2, students form pairs and discuss their ideas with a partner. In step 3, the teacher calls students at random to report their pair's thinking to the class.

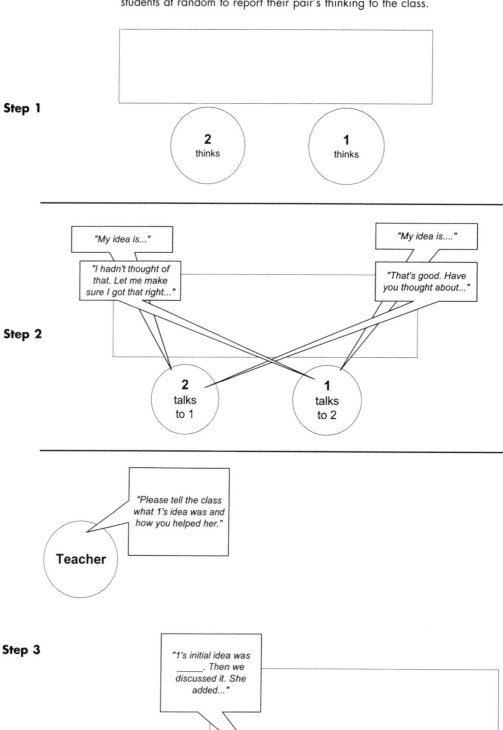

team, the same number of points as my groupmate who always gets 100 on quizzes.

Some teachers worry that if they use STAD, they will be spending all their time calculating averages and improvement points. Here are a few ideas about how to make this easier:

- Let students do some of the calculating.
- Use a computer spreadsheet.
- Recalculate students' average periodically (e.g., every 5 weeks) instead of after each quiz.

THINK–PAIR–SHARE

Think–Pair–Share is one of the best-known CL techniques (see Figure 3.2).

Step 1. Students are in pairs. The teacher asks a question. Each student spends time to *think* alone. (To encourage students to think, not talk, during this time, Louisa Leong, a first-grade teacher we know, asks students to close their eyes.)

Step 2. Members of each *pair* discuss with each other what they have learned.

Step 3. The teacher calls students at random. These students *share* about their pair's discussion. (Students may need reminding to share what their partner said or what evolved from the pair's discussion, rather than focusing on their own ideas.)

How Does Think–Pair–Share Help?

Two ways that Think–Pair–Share improves group functioning are as follows:

The think step recognizes more reflective students who prefer to have time to think before talking, although all students can benefit from a chance to think for a bit.

The share step encourages students to listen carefully and to be sure they've understood their partner.

Let's look at how Think–Pair–Share promotes positive interdependence. First, is a gain for one a gain for another? Yes, because if I can help my partner contribute good ideas, that means I've got better ideas to share if I'm called on. Second, is help needed, or can the task be done alone? The task cannot be done alone, because if I am called on, I need to report on the discussion that occurred with my partner, not just on my ideas.

Think–Pair–Share is best thought of not as a single CL technique but as the starting point for a wide range of complementary techniques. For instance, instead of *think* as the 1st step, we can substitute *write* and have Write–Pair–Share. Writing helps students remember their ideas and pushes them to get going and think; otherwise, their paper will be blank.

Figure 3.3 Write–Pair–Switch is similar to Think–Pair–Share. In step 1, each student writes his or her own response to a question asked by the teacher. In step 2, students form pairs and discuss their ideas with a partner. In step 3, students switch partners to form new pairs and tell their new partners about the ideas of their former partners.

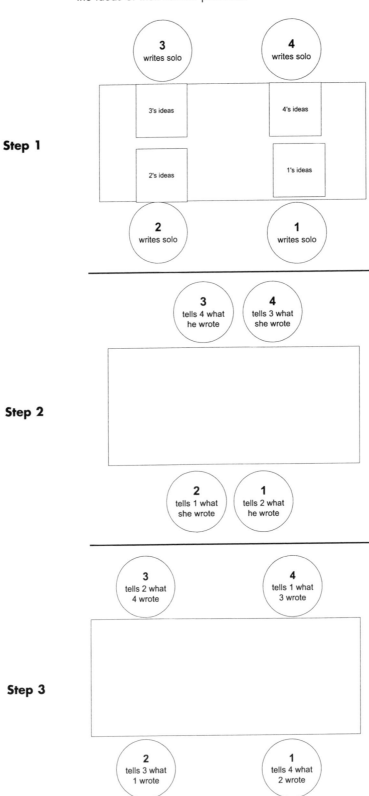

In addition to think and write, other 1st steps could be draw, observe, smell, search (the library, the Internet, or other sources), and visualize.

Many alternatives exist for the share step as well. Actually, the word *share* may be confusing because it's not clear with whom the sharing is to be done. Think–Pair–Class might be more descriptive. Besides sharing with the class, pairs can also share with the other pair in their foursome. Spencer Kagan (1994) calls this *Think–Pair–Square*, because squares have four sides.

A high school English teacher, Pearly Tan (personal communication, May 1995), developed an alternative to Square. Instead of one pair reporting to the other, students switch partners. For the Think–Pair, 1 and 2 are a pair and 3 and 4 are a pair. Then, students switch, and 1 and 3, and 2 and 4, are partners. We call this *Think–Pair–Switch, Draw–Pair–Switch*, and so forth.

And, why stop at just 3 steps? Why not have Draw–Pair–Switch–Draw, and so forth? We hope that what students draw the second time differs from what they drew the first time due to the interaction they've had with their first and second partners.

One more point worth making about the Think–Pair–Share family of techniques is that they can take just a short amount of time to do. For example, students think for 1 minute, pair for 2 minutes, and then the teacher takes about 2 minutes to call on a few students to share about their pair's discussion. A total of just 5 minutes! In fact, many other CL techniques can be done quickly, for example, Ask Your Neighbor (Chapter 4). By using short CL techniques, we can easily combine CL with lectures, demonstrations, videos, CD-ROMs, and individual work.

WRITE–PAIR–SWITCH

Write–Pair–Switch (see Figure 3.3) is one of the techniques that grew out of Think–Pair–Share.

- Each student works alone to *write* a response to a question or other prompt.
- Students *pair* and discuss their responses.
- Students *switch* partners and form a new pair with a member of the other pair in their group of four. Students tell their new partner about their former partner's response.

Example of a Write–Pair–Switch Activity in a Science Lesson

Individual students describe one change they would like to see in humans' use of resources, such as paper or oil, and why that change would be beneficial. They describe their change to a partner and try to convince the partner that the change would be beneficial. Students switch partners and describe and justify their former partner's change to their new partner.

COMING ATTRACTIONS

Positive interdependence provides group members with a feeling of support. They know that their groupmates are there for them. But some students may be tempted to lie back and let their groupmates do the work for them. Thus, besides support, students also might benefit from a bit of pressure. This pressure is provided in the form of the CL principle of Individual Accountability, which is highlighted in Chapter 4.

4

Principle: Individual Accountability

KEY QUESTIONS

How can I encourage all students to participate and learn?

How can I help students learn to take responsibility for their group?

COOPERATIVE LEARNING TECHNIQUES INTRODUCED IN THIS CHAPTER

Circle of Writers

Circle of Speakers

Before and After

Focused Discussion Pairs

Ask Your Neighbor

INDIVIDUAL ACCOUNTABILITY

One of the most frequent concerns about the use of group activities is that one or two of the group members will try to do as little as they can, taking advantage of their hard-working groupmates. These hitchhiking students not only limit their own opportunity to learn, they limit their teammates' success as well by depriving them of additional ideas and energy and hurting the group's morale. The CL principle of Individual Accountability provides us with some ways to address this very real problem.

Individual accountability means that each participant is responsible for contributing to the learning and success of the group. Each student feels responsible to contribute to the group, to learn, and to publicly demonstrate competence. Kagan (1998) defines individual accountability as being when an individual public performance is required of all group members. This does not mean standing on a stage in an auditorium and singing the national anthem. All it means is that students need to let at least one other person in their group know—via speaking, writing, drawing, and so forth—what they think about the topic being discussed. In other words, for our purposes, *public* can refer to an audience of a single person. When students say what's in their minds or write it for others to read, it is now public and no longer private, which puts pressure on students to think and to learn so that their public performance can be a good one.

Perhaps more important, this public performance allows groupmates to learn from each other. By listening to and observing others' performances, students can benefit from their peers' strengths and weaknesses. Students can compliment each other on their strengths, taking these as positive examples to learn from. When students help each other overcome areas of weakness, the helper benefits as well because, as mentioned in Chapter 2, the saying is, "Those who teach learn twice." Also, as one teacher put it after a CL lesson, "When students taught each other, I myself learned new ways of communicating the concepts. Which is great! Kids have their own ways of explaining things to each other, sometimes more effectively than we teachers."

These public performances also help teachers better understand what students are thinking. Being able to listen in as students explain concepts to one another is a much better way to monitor learning than standing in front of the class and lecturing, trying to guess from the look on students' faces what's going on in their minds.

Building Individual Accountability

CL techniques attempt to encourage individual accountability by various means, such as these activities:

- Individual group members share their ideas with one or more of their groupmates. This can be done orally, in writing, or in other forms. This is what happens in Write–Pair–Switch (Chapter 3) and similar CL techniques.
- Each group member has a part in the group product. This product can be oral, such as a part in a role play, or written, such as writing a section of a report. An example here is projects (see Chapter 8).
- We call on students at random to tell and explain what their group has done, as in Numbered Heads Together (Chapter 5).
- Each group member has a role. If that role is not carried out, group effectiveness suffers. (See Chapter 6 for details on roles.)

- Students share with their group what they have learned elsewhere, as in Jigsaw (Chapter 3), or share with another group, as in Traveling Heads Together (Chapter 5).
- Each student takes an individual quiz or test, as in Before and After (below).

SPECIFIC TECHNIQUES

Let's look at several CL techniques and see how they promote individual accountability.

Circle of Writers

A simple and very versatile CL technique is Circle of Writers. This can be done in foursomes or pairs. In Circle of Writers, each group member takes a turn to write. Circle of Writers can be done two ways. In Circle of Writers (All at Once), each student has a piece of paper, and all group members write simultaneously (see Figure 4.1). As a conclusion, we can call on a few students to share with the class what was written in their group.

Here are some examples of how Circle of Writers (All at Once) works.

Language Arts. Each student begins writing a story. After a designated amount of time, for example, 4 minutes, individual students pass their story to the person on the left, who reads what has been written so far and continues that story. This keeps going until the stories return to the person who started them. Students then write endings for the story they initiated.

Mathematics. Each group member is given a separate, multistep math problem. Each student does one step and then passes the paper to the person on the right, who does the next step. This continues until the solution is completed. If students think a step has been done incorrectly, they can call a time-out. During the time-out, the group discusses, and tries to reach consensus on, how the step should be done. (Perhaps more than one way may be correct.)

Science. Each group member begins with the name of a different insect. The group's task is to show the life cycle of each of the insects. They each do a drawing, or select a drawing from a common pool, that shows the first stage in the life cycle of their insect. The paper passes to the person on the left, who does a drawing, or selects the drawing, of the second stage. This continues until the life cycles of all four insects are completed.

Social Studies. Each student has a blank table dealing with advantages of communications media such as TV and newspapers. There are, say, 16 cells in the table. Each group member takes a turn to fill in one cell of the table before passing the paper to the left.

Figure 4.1   In Circle of Writers (All at Once), each student has her or his own piece of paper. In step 1, all group members write simultaneously. In step 2, students pass their piece of paper to the student on the left, who adds new material to the original writer's contribution. This process continues (step 3) until each piece of paper has a contribution from each group member and is returned to its original writer (step 4). In step 5, the teacher may call on a few individual students to report about what they wrote and what other group members contributed.

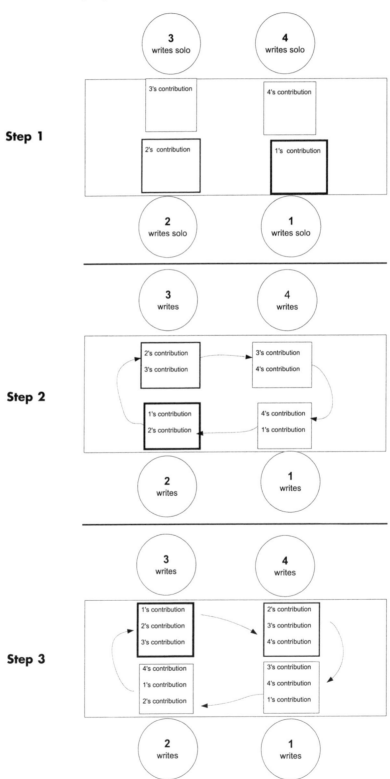

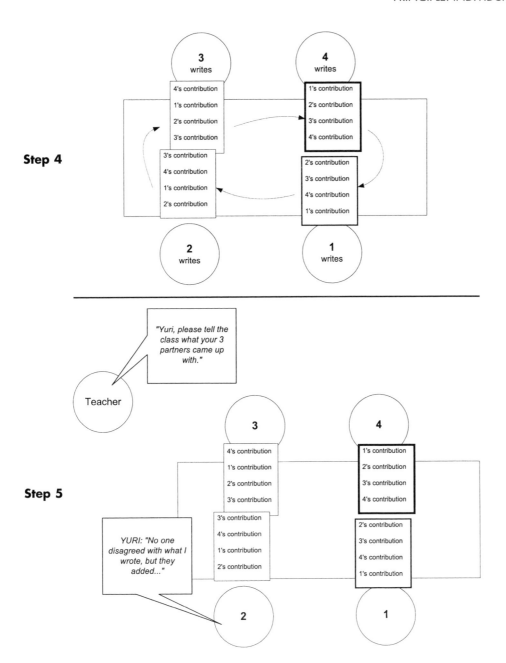

In another version, Circle of Writers (Take Turns), our group of four has only one piece of paper, and group members take turns to write (see Figure 4.2). As a conclusion, we can call on a few students to share with the class what was written in their group.

Circle of Writers (Take Turns) might be used in the same examples as those given for the All-at-Once version, but one question we need to ask ourselves when deciding which form of Circle of Writers to use is how long individual students will take to write their part before passing the paper. If each student is going to write for 4 minutes before passing the paper, in a group of four, students are inactive for 12 minutes before the paper comes back to them. Waiting time can also be reduced by doing Circle of Writers (Take Turns) in groups of two rather than in foursomes.

Figure 4.2   In Circle of Writers (Take Turns), the group has only one piece of paper, and group members take turns writing, which makes this activity better suited for shorter contributions. In step 1, one group member writes solo while the others brainstorm. In step 2, the next group member receives the original piece of paper and adds a personal contribution. This process continues (step 3) until each member of the group has added a contribution, and the piece of paper returns to the first writer (step 4). In step 5, the teacher may call on a few individual students to report on what their group wrote.

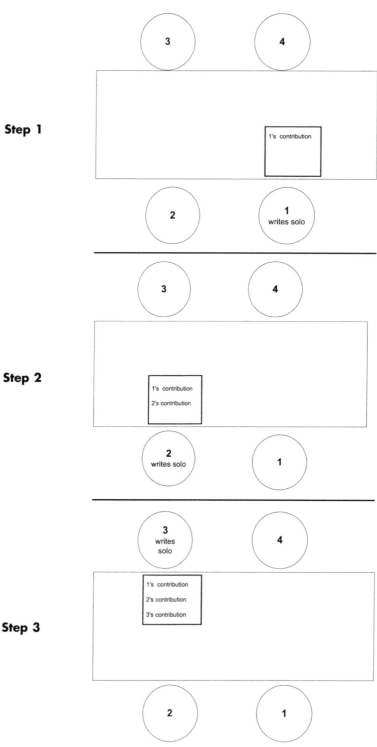

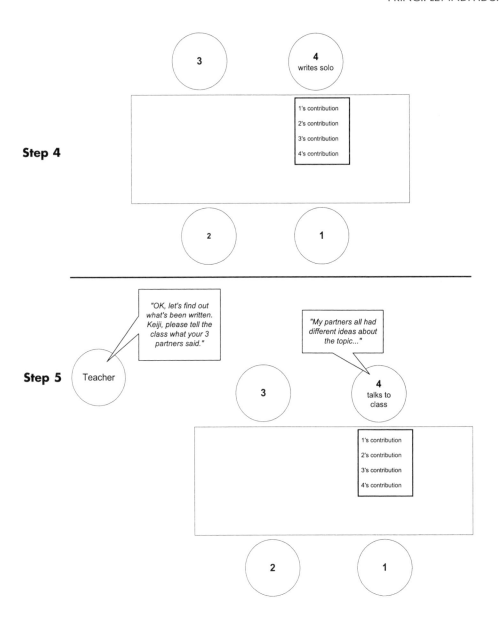

Here are some cases where we might choose Circle of Writers (Take Turns):

- Students make a list of descriptive adjectives suitable for a particular topic or to describe a picture. (It is always good to have a supply of pictures from publications such as *National Geographic* to serve as idea starters for activities.)
- Each student writes an adjective and then passes the paper. Groups can do multiple rounds, with a different type of adjective each time—color adjectives, size adjectives, shape adjectives, and so forth.
- Students brainstorm uses for discarded newspapers. While one student is writing, the others can be thinking of ideas or illustrating their ideas.

- Students label the parts of the digestive system and their functions on a drawing.
- Students create an illustrated story (like a comic book) through drawing in sequence (just quick drafts, otherwise students have to wait too long for their turns). In a second round, students could write captions or dialog for the cartoon drawings.
- Students make a list of observations of an object. Each student writes an observation and passes the paper. The next person checks that it is an observation and not an inference and writes another observation.
- Students generate questions they have about the lesson they have just completed. These can be things they did not fully understand or things they want to know more about. This is a valuable source of feedback to the teacher on what will need to be retaught or reviewed.

Circle of Speakers

A variation on Circle of Writers (Take Turns) is Circle of Speakers. Each group member takes a turn to speak. Obviously, we wouldn't want to recommend Circle of Speakers (All at Once), because then there would be nobody listening, although we have seen groups that seemed to be attempting this. In Circle of Writers and Circle of Speakers, individual accountability is promoted by the fact that individual group members are asked to give an individual public performance by writing or speaking their ideas. Groupmates view or hear these ideas as papers get passed around or ideas are spoken.

Before and After

Before and After is a good CL technique to check students' mastery of content, for example, in preparation for a test. It builds individual accountability because students have to participate in the group work to do well on the quiz (a public performance).

Step 1. Before starting a new unit or topic, the teacher prepares a quiz on key points to be covered. Students take this *before quiz*. Groupmates score each other's quizzes. The teacher records the scores with particular attention to the items missed by more than a few students. Students and teachers highlight the information and skills involved in items missed on the quiz.

Step 2. The class studies the topic or unit in preparation for a similar quiz, the *after quiz*. The after quiz may be a combination of student- and teacher-generated items. Students study as a group but take the quiz individually.

Step 3. After completing the after quiz, students again score each other's papers within their group. Before and after scores are compared.

Groups highlight areas in which members have improved as well as areas in which further improvement is needed.

Step 4. Groups with higher after scores can celebrate by, for example, doing their team cheer, or another kind of reward can be used.

Variation. Some types of quiz questions may be difficult for students to score, in which case the teacher needs to score them or help students to do so.

Before and After promotes individual accountability because students give individual public performances on the before-and-after quizzes. Another advantage of the technique is that the before quiz highlights key ideas that the teacher feels students need to learn, and the after quiz alerts students to what the teacher hopes they will recall from the unit they just studied.

Focused Discussion Pairs (Johnson & Johnson, 1991)

Focused Discussion Pairs is a good technique for highlighting the maxim "two heads are better than one" and for building a sense of responsibility to one's partner. The technique works like this:

Step 1. The teacher asks a question. Individual members of a pair come up with an answer on their own.

Step 2. Partners share their answers with each other.

Step 3. The pairs work together to try to develop an answer that is better than either member's initial response to the question.

Step 4. Both members of the pair need to be able to present their new answer and to explain the thinking behind it.

Step 5. The teacher calls on individual students at random to share the answer they and their partner developed.

Clearly, Focused Discussion Pairs works best with thinking questions, not yes or no questions or those that have only one, simple, correct answer. After students develop their individual answers, they do individual public performances by sharing their answers with their partner (the partner is the public). In step 5, they need to be ready to do another individual public performance if the teacher calls on them. Here are some examples of how Focused Discussion Pairs can be used in different subject areas:

Language Arts. Answering a set of questions after reading a text or section of a novel.

Mathematics. Solving a set of equations.

Science. Planning an investigation to ensure a fair test as part of a laboratory experiment.

Social Studies. Speculating on how history would have been different if a particular event, for example, dropping of atomic bombs during World War II, had not taken place.

Ask Your Neighbor

Ask Your Neighbor (Figure 4.3) is a quick and easy technique that requires students to communicate effectively with their partners both as speakers and listeners.

Step 1. The teacher asks the whole class a question. Rather than listening to students' answers right away, the teacher requests students to "Ask

Figure 4.3 Ask Your Neighbor encourages careful listening. In step 1, the teacher asks the class a question but requests that students "ask your neighbor" before replying. In step 2, the teacher calls on students randomly, asking them to report what their neighbor said.

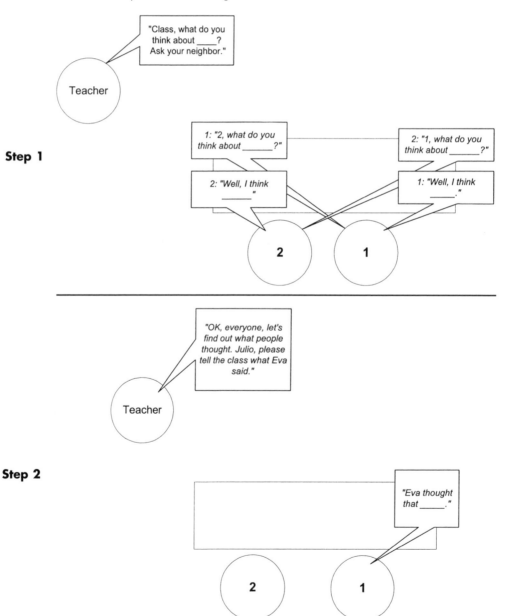

your neighbor!" Students turn to the other member of their pair. Each person is either number 1 or number 2. Number 1 asks the teacher's question (or one of her or his own) of number 2. Number 2 has, say, 1 minute to answer. Then, they reverse roles.

Step 2. The teacher calls on students randomly, asking, "What did your neighbor say?" This encourages students to help their partners think of something to say and to listen carefully to their partners, or they will be stuck if the teacher calls on them.

In order to make full use of the allotted time, students may want to elaborate on their answers with support for their ideas, and partners may want to ask follow-up questions. All pupils give an individual public performance as they respond to their partner. And they need to be ready to tell the class what their partner told them. This is a good technique to develop listening skills as well as oral skills.

COMING ATTRACTIONS

One very effective way to encourage individual accountability is via assessment. Strategies for assessing students when CL is used are discussed in Chapter 9, but as a quick example, in the CL technique STAD (Chapter 3), students study together but take quizzes alone. CL gives students many opportunities to give individual public performances because CL promotes Simultaneous Interaction. This principle is explained in our next chapter, Chapter 5.

5

Principle: Simultaneous Interaction

KEY QUESTIONS

How can I give students lots of opportunities to express their ideas?

Should students report on their group work to the whole class?

How can I encourage students to explain their thinking to their group?

COOPERATIVE LEARNING TECHNIQUES INTRODUCED IN THIS CHAPTER

Review Pairs

Numbered Heads Together

Traveling Heads Together

Carousel

SIMULTANEOUS INTERACTION

As noted in Chapter 2, Deci and Ryan (1985) highlight three basic human needs—relatedness, competence, and autonomy. We discussed relatedness in Chapter 2. Now let's consider competence. Cooperative learning promotes competence by putting students into a supportive learning environment in which they have groupmates who can help them to try out new ideas and give them constructive feedback in a low-risk setting. Working with their group motivates students to increase their competence. Furthermore, students demonstrate their competence both by mastering the material and by helping their groupmates. By increasing the support students have, we increase students' chances of success, and this leads to higher levels of confidence and competence.

Interaction among students, whether spoken or written, builds competence. This interaction is missing in classrooms where students spend the majority of their time listening to the teacher or to the one student selected by the teacher. This is why simultaneous interaction is such an important CL principle.

According to Kagan (1998), to know whether simultaneous interaction is present, we look around the classroom and ask ourselves, "What percentage of the entire class is overtly active at the same time?" Being overtly active means speaking, writing, or performing a hands-on task. When students work in foursomes, and one student per foursome is talking or writing, as in Circle of Speakers or Circle of Writers, 25 percent of the class is overtly active. When students work in pairs doing Circle of Speakers or Circle of Writers, one student per pair is talking or writing, so 50 percent of the class is overtly active.

Why *overtly*? Listening and reading also involve a great deal of mental activity. The difference lies in the fact that when students speak and write, they are pushed to put their ideas into words for others to hear or see, thus promoting individual accountability (Chapter 4). Having students put their ideas into words offers three advantages:

- It allows peers to benefit from one another's ideas.
- It helps students to clarify, and perhaps notice gaps in, their thinking as they try to put ideas into words.
- It provides us teachers with insight into what's going on between the students' ears.

Sequential Interaction

The opposite of simultaneous interaction is sequential interaction, the pattern that is the hallmark of teacher-fronted classrooms. Teachers do most of the talking, and when we do call on students, we call on them one at a time, *sequentially*. We ask a question, call a student to answer, evaluate the answer, talk a bit more, call another student, and so on. A story we heard about an elementary school language arts class aptly demonstrates the dominance of teacher talk:

One day, the lesson was on descriptive adjectives. The teacher wrote a couple of such adjectives on the board—*helpful* and *easygoing*—and pointed out a couple of students in the class who had been particularly helpful lately and a couple of others who were particularly easygoing. Next, the teacher wrote *talkative* on the board. She asked the students, "In this entire class, who is the most talkative of them all?" In the back of the class, a few of the more mischievous students raised their hands and chorused, "The teacher."

Sadly, this story is all too typical. The person in the classroom who needs the least practice explaining things to others, the teacher, is the one who gets the most practice.

What percentage of the entire class is overtly active when we use teacher-fronted instruction and we call on one student at a time to speak? In a class of 25, this is 4 percent. By adding group activities to the classroom mix, we dramatically increase the amount of overt student activity. For instance, we can do direct instruction for 10 minutes and then ask students to do a Think–Pair–Switch (Chapter 3).

Applying Simultaneous Interaction

What about having students report on the work of their group?

Simultaneous interaction encourages us to make CL a regular part of our teaching. It also encourages us to examine how we do CL. For instance, after students have worked in groups, they often want to have their work validated by reporting to the entire class and the teacher. We also want a way to check what students have done and provide feedback. Thus the temptation exists to have representatives from each group stand up, perhaps even come to the front of the class, and report on what their group has done.

Where has the simultaneous interaction gone when this takes place? We're back to sequential interaction. And what are the other groups doing during these presentations? It's very likely that groups that have yet to present are busy preparing. They're not paying attention. Those groups that have finished presenting are relaxing. They're not paying attention either. Who can blame them? Who wants to listen to so many presentations on the same topic?

As an alternative, we recommend not calling too many groups to present. Instead, one group or its representative can present to another group. There are a number of CL techniques, such as Carousel (described later in this chapter), that help maintain simultaneous interaction while students do presentations. Another way to make presentations more interesting is for all groups to work on the same topic, but for each group to take on a different aspect of that topic. Similarly, if students are doing the same basic task, such as working on a particular type of mathematics problem, each group can have different examples of that type of problem. Also, when groups do present to the entire class, if they involve their classmates in CL activities related to the content of their presentation, the whole class is more likely to be attentive and engaged. See Chapter 8 for more ideas on this.

Why Is Interaction Important?

We have looked at the *simultaneous* part of simultaneous interaction. Now, let's examine the *interaction* part. Interaction is what makes CL exciting for both students and teachers, where students push each other to develop new insights and skills. Too often in group work, we see students sitting together but not working together, not interacting. Sometimes, division of labor can also stifle interaction. If each group member is responsible for doing one part of a task, we need to encourage groups to interact so as to provide feedback and to learn from the work of all the group members.

CL offers many tools for promoting interaction. For instance, Resource Positive Interdependence (Chapter 3), in which each group member has unique information or materials, pushes students to share because they realize that no one member can do the task alone. Equal Participation (Chapter 6) fosters interaction by structuring for participation by all members. In Chapter 4, we looked at individual accountability, which pushes all group members to share their ideas with others. Classbuilding (Chapter 1) and teambuilding (Chapter 2) also help create an environment in which students feel comfortable with, and care about, groupmates and other classmates.

Nonetheless, we need to realize that all teachers can do is encourage and promote interaction; we can't guarantee it. In the same way, neither can we prevent unwanted interaction, such as when students are supposed to be taking a test individually, but one student risks getting in trouble to help a classmate. Appreciating our powerful, yet limited, role represents an important understanding for teachers. It's the same understanding we need to appreciate that learning, in the final analysis, is based on what goes on in the heads of our students, not on what we say to them or give them to read. All the more reason that we need to hone our skills as a guide on the side rather than as a sage on a stage. CL helps us do this.

TECHNIQUES FOR PROMOTING SIMULTANEOUS INTERACTION

Activities discussed in Chapter 3, such as Write–Pair–Square and Think–Pair–Switch, as contrasted to Write–Pair–Share or Think–Pair–Share, offer ways of maintaining simultaneous interaction. This is because the *share* step, in which students take turns to report to the entire class, involves sequential interaction. In contrast, Square, in which pairs report to each other, or Switch, in which partners change pair mates, can keep the simultaneous interaction going. Now we will look at some other CL activities that help maintain simultaneous interaction.

Review Pairs (Johnson & Johnson, 1991)

Having students think aloud offers a great way to promote deeper understanding and to help students learn from their groupmates. It also calls upon the collaborative skill of giving reasons for what we do (Chapter 7). While thinking aloud can be added to many CL techniques, Review Pairs (see Figure 5.1) is one CL technique specifically designed to include thinking aloud. Here's how it works.

Step 1. Each group of four begins working as two pairs. Each pair has the same list of problems or questions. Partner 1 (the thinker) in each group reads the first problem or question and thinks aloud (verbalizes her or his thinking) as the pair works on it. Partner 2 (the coach) listens, watches, and coaches. Coaching includes giving suggestions and encouragement as well as asking questions. Coaching does *not* include pointing out every mistake as soon as it is made or doing the task for the partner.

Step 2. Partners reverse the roles of thinker and coach for the second problem or question.

Step 3. After every two problems or questions, the two pairs in the foursome get together to discuss their responses and try to reach consensus.

After the discussion, the pairs thank each other for their ideas and continue with the next two problems or questions.

Note: Although the name of the CL technique is Review Pairs, this does not mean that students can only use it for review. The think-aloud aspect of the technique makes it useful for any type of learning.

Examples of Review Pairs

Here are some examples of how Review Pairs can be used in various areas of the curriculum:

Language Arts. Students think aloud as they answer questions about a literary passage that requires analysis.

Mathematics. Students try to solve a set of similar, multistep problems—ideally, ones that have more than one solution. They think aloud about how they can represent the problem, for instance, using drawings or objects such as counters. When they switch roles, the second thinker can address the challenge of finding alternative ways of solving the problems.

Science. After doing an investigation and obtaining data, students think aloud about what their results mean. For example, the teacher gives them three leaves. They test them for starch and find one leaf tests positive, one tests negative, and one tests positive in some areas and negative in other areas. Then members of the pair take turns thinking aloud about the reasons that this might be so.

Social Studies. Students do problems involving distributing limited resources and think aloud as they figure out the most equitable solutions.

Figure 5.1 In Review Pairs, each group of four students receives a list of questions. In step 1, the foursome works in pairs. Each pair has a *thinker* and a *coach* who work together to answer the first question on their list. In step 2, each pair reverses thinker and coach roles as they work on the second question. In step 3, after every two problems or questions, the foursome gets together to discuss their responses and try to reach consensus.

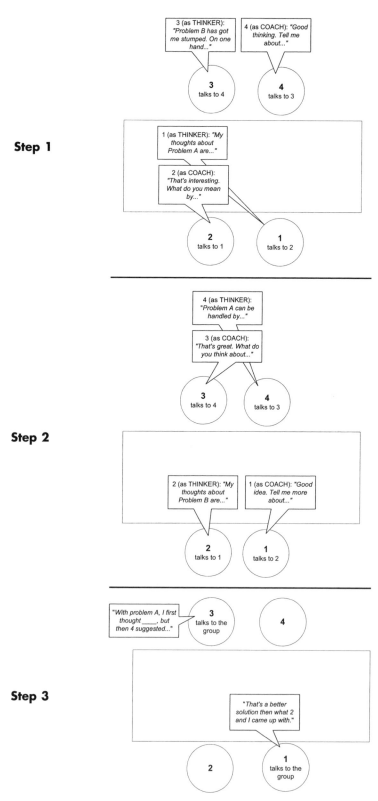

Numbered Heads Together (Kagan, 1994)

Numbered Heads Together is a well-known CL technique. It works like this:

Step 1. Students in foursomes each have a number—1, 2, 3, or 4.

Step 2. The teacher asks a question or gives a task.

Step 3. Groups put their heads together to respond to the problem or do the task.

Step 4. The teacher calls a number, and the student in each group with that number gives and explains their group's response or work.

Traveling Heads Together (Kagan, 1994)

This technique takes Numbered Heads Together on the road. You will note that the last step of Numbered Heads Together gets us back to sequential interaction, because one student is giving and explaining their group's answer to the entire class; that is, one person at a time talks. Thus in a class of 25, only 4 percent of the class is overtly active.

Traveling Heads Together works to restore simultaneous interaction. Here's how: The students whose number is called, let's say the 2's, move to another group. There, they give and explain their home group's answer to the group they are visiting. Thus, rather than just one student, 25 percent of the class is overtly active.

The Importance of Explanations

Please note that in step 4, students give and *explain* their group's answer and don't just present it. Explanations are very important. Learning happens best if students understand the thinking behind the answer. It's a bit like the saying, "Give people wheat, and they eat for a day. Teach them how to grow wheat, and they eat for a lifetime." Explaining to others crystallizes one's own thoughts so that knowledge can be internalized.

The crucial nature of explanations is illustrated by this adaptation of a story told by Johnson (1989):

A psychologist had been working with three patients for about a year and felt they were finally ready to be released from treatment. But she wanted to be sure, so she called them into her office and said, "I'm proud of the progress the three of you have made. If you can answer this simple question, you can all go home."

The psychologist turned to Patient A and asked, "What is three times three?" to which the patient responded, "Monday." The psychologist was thunderstruck. Hiding her disappointment, she quickly turned to Patient B and repeated her question, to which Patient B replied "Mangoes." Her knees buckling, the psychologist looked beseechingly at Patient C and asked, "Please, you know what three times three is, don't you?" The last patient promptly replied, "Nine."

A huge smile of relief spread across the psychologist's face. Then, she got a bright idea. "Would you mind," she asked Patient C, "explaining to our two friends why three times three equals nine?" "My pleasure," replied Patient C, "Three times three equals nine because Monday times mangoes equals nine."

Carousel (Kagan, 1994)

Carousel (see Figure 5.2) is another good technique for facilitating simultaneous interaction.

Step 1. Groups do an extended task, such as a project (Chapter 8), a graphic, an experiment, or a skit, in which some kind of product is produced.

Step 2. Groups take turns to rotate around the room to read, watch, and experience other groups' products. They also give feedback. This feedback can be spoken or written and can be given in such forms as notes attached to a display or written in a space left especially for that purpose.

Step 3. Groups use what they've learned from their tour of the classroom to improve their own product.

How can you encourage students to be accountable during Carousel? Although Carousel can produce a lot of activity, it's possible that some students just wander around. Here are several ways to encourage individual accountability during Carousel:

Figure 5.2 Carousel facilitates simultaneous interaction as students rotate around the room to listen to, observe, and discuss the work of other groups.

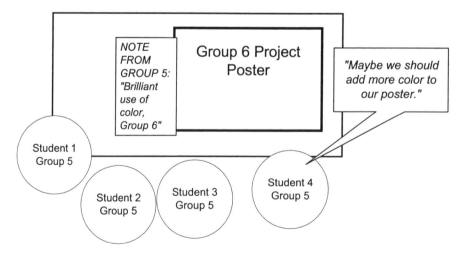

- Individual group members can have a part in presenting their group's work to other groups, for example, if the group does some kind of performance, such as singing a song.
- Group members can rotate the role of the person who stays behind to explain and take questions about the group's product, for instance, a poster. (If the group is doing a performance, such as a skit, for which everyone is needed, such rotation will not be possible.)
- In step 2, students can take turns to give their group's feedback to the groups they visit.
- In step 3, groups can use Circle of Speakers to discuss the feedback they receive from other groups and what they've learned from other groups' products, before deciding how they might improve their own product.

COMING ATTRACTIONS

By bearing in mind the CL principle of Simultaneous Interaction, we encourage large amounts of student participation. However, when groups function poorly, this participation is often very unequal. That is why the CL principle of Equal Participation is the focus of Chapter 6.

6

Principle: Equal Participation

KEY QUESTIONS

How can I promote equal participation in groups?

How might CL help with differences in student ability levels?

What about the students whose main strengths do not lie in academic skills?

COOPERATIVE LEARNING TECHNIQUES INTRODUCED IN THIS CHAPTER

Talking Chips

Web of Talk

Music as Content Carrier

Group Mind Mapping

Draw–Pair–Switch

EQUAL PARTICIPATION

When students work in groups, it's not uncommon that some of the members take over, dominating the discussions and work, while others are left out. This problem is addressed by this chapter's cooperative learning

(CL) principle—Equal Participation. First off, we should recognize that it's not realistic to insist on absolutely equal participation. On any particular topic or task, there are many legitimate reasons why one student or another has more or less to contribute. However, as we discussed in Chapters 4 and 5, participation represents a key to learning. It is cause for concern if any group members consistently participate less. Thus, as Kagan (1998) suggests, we should always be looking at the groups and asking, "How equal is the participation?"

Many CL techniques offer ways to promote equal participation. For instance, Circle of Speakers and Circle of Writers both facilitate a turn for each group member. Nonetheless, we can't be sure that just because students have the opportunity to take turns, they will take their turns or use them effectively. To encourage each student to take the initiative to participate, collaborative skills have to be developed (Chapter 7). Groupmates need to learn how to encourage others to participate by, for example, asking a question or giving a hint.

Particularly as the typical classroom becomes more multicultural, we have students with a much greater diversity of backgrounds and styles of interaction. Although this represents a challenge, the increased diversity of the classroom is a tremendous resource for learning through shared experiences and perspectives. CL can be a helpful tool in maximizing these new learning opportunities. As Slavin (1995) states, "Cooperative learning can help make diversity a resource rather than a problem" (p. 3).

Roles in Cooperative Learning

The most commonly used means of equalizing participation in CL is assigning specific roles and responsibilities to each group member. This relates to Role Positive Interdependence (Chapter 3). Students can play many possible roles; the choice will depend on the CL activity and the instructional objectives. Here are some of the more popular roles:

- **Facilitator** (also called **Coach**): keeps the group on task and makes sure everyone knows what the instructions are.
- **Timekeeper:** keeps track of the time limits.
- **Checker:** checks to see that all group members have understood.
- **Encourager** (also called **Cheerleader**): encourages everyone to participate and leads the celebration of success.
- **Recorder:** keeps notes on what the group has discussed; these can be in normal note form or in the shape of graphic organizers, such as word webs or mind maps.
- **Reporter:** reports the group's work to other groups or the whole class.
- **Materials Manager:** makes sure that the group has the materials it needs and that these are properly taken care of.
- **Questioner:** asks questions to prompt the group to go more deeply and broadly into their task.

- **Summarizer:** highlights the main things the group has discussed and keeps track of the group's progress.
- **Paraphraser:** restates what the previous speaker said, to check comprehension.
- **Praiser:** compliments groupmates for their ideas and their role in the group.
- **Elaborator:** connects the group's ideas to other things they have studied or to out-of-school contexts (see SUMMER in Chapter 7, the Elaborate step).
- **Safety Monitor:** helps to see that safety procedures are followed when groups use potentially dangerous equipment.
- **Conflict Creator:** plays the role of devil's advocate, bringing out opposing points of view and other possibilities, as well as unearthing the conflicting ideas that are already in the group but that are being unexpressed or ignored.
- **Sound Hound:** makes sure the noise level does not go too high.
- **Observer:** notes how the group is working together (see Chapter 7 for more on monitoring group functioning).

To facilitate learning their roles, students can master certain phrases or gambits that go with a particular role. For instance, Encouragers use phrases such as

"What do you think about that?"

"You've got lots of good ideas."

"I think we're going in the right direction! What's next?"

These gambits can be accompanied by a list of behaviors that go with each role. For instance, the behaviors of the Facilitator could include

- Keeping group on task
- Making sure everyone understands what to do
- Checking to be sure people do their assigned tasks
- Helping to resolve disputes among members
- Suggesting what the group should do next

Sometimes it is important to give students official support for playing their roles, just as we have official support to play our role as teacher. For instance, when students who are not popular with their classmates play the role of Facilitator, other students may hesitate to accept them, and it may be difficult for low-status students to assert their authority and play their role without the teacher's backing. Official support can be provided in such ways as these:

- Individual students have laminated cards or table tents (tent cards) with the name of their role on one side and, perhaps, a list of behaviors and set phrases on the other.

- Each group member has a number. The roles for each number appear on the board; for example, all the 1's are Checkers, 2's are Facilitators, 3's are Questioners, and 4's are Sound Hounds.
- Students wear distinctive badges with their roles stated on them.

The use of roles fits with the concept of distributed leadership, which Dishon and O'Leary (1993) make their cooperative learning principle number one. The idea is that there is no one leader selected by the teacher or the group. Instead, everyone acts as a leader, whatever roles they play. Leadership can be shown in different ways. The Timekeeper, the member who reminds the group about the time limit, is a leader—as is the Questioner, the member who asks questions such as, "Why is this a good answer?"

Should Students Always Take the Same Role?

Teachers and students often find it easier for students always to play a particular role that fits their temperament and skills, but this should be avoided. Roles should rotate so that everyone has opportunities to try out each role. This differs from the situation in the work world, where the emphasis normally resides in getting the job done as well and as quickly as possible. In education, quality and speed still demand attention. But goal number one is the development of each individual pupil.

It should be clear to students that roles will rotate and that everyone will have chances to play all the different roles. To do this, teachers or groups can keep records of which roles each group member has already played.

The fact that one group member has been assigned a particular role, such as Checker, doesn't mean that others cannot play the same role. After all, who's going to check that the Checker understands? Similarly, students should be participating as regular group members, in addition to performing their roles. This is likely to take a bit of practice.

A common misconception about CL is that the focus is always on the group. In fact, as Johnson and Johnson (1998) point out, the focus is on the individual and how groups can support the development of their individual members. Thus if a group has worked together and come up with perfect answers to a set of math problems, or conducted and written up a science experiment very well, the group's work is not yet finished. Their work isn't finished until each member of that group can correctly do the problems or conduct and write up the experiment well. Maybe each member couldn't do it as well as the group—after all "We is greater than I"—but, still, each member should be able to explain what the group did and how they did it and be able to do a reasonable job on their own, according to their individual past achievement and personal goals.

A negative example of this occurred when one of the authors of this book attended a workshop on using CL with computers. His team was given the task of doing a PowerPoint presentation. The role of Hardware

Handler (who makes sure the equipment is taken care of) was given to someone whose real-life job was maintaining the computer lab where the workshop was being held. The role of Keyboard Captain (who uses the computer to input and manipulate the group's ideas) was given to someone who was a PowerPoint wizard. The role of Composer (who comes up with the ideas to put into the computer) was given to the person who was an English teacher, and the only native English speaker of the three, but who knew nothing about PowerPoint and little about hardware. The group came up with a fairly good product in a fairly short time, but it failed miserably in the larger goal of increasing each group member's skills.

What About Students Who Are Second-Language Learners?

When there is a mixture of language proficiency among students, as in a class with some students who are second-language speakers, we can assign the less-proficient students a role that does not require much language, such as Timekeeper or Materials Manager. As these students improve their language ability, they can move gradually into roles that require more fluency. Providing these students an important role to play in the group will keep them engaged and motivated, contribute to their language development, and bolster their relations with groupmates.

TECHNIQUES THAT ENCOURAGE EQUAL PARTICIPATION

One way to address the issue of equal participation is for students to see for themselves that equal participation is often lacking in their groups. The next two games help raise students' awareness of the issue.

Talking Chips (Kagan, 1994)

Talking Chips is a good technique for encouraging all group members to participate (see Figure 6.1).

Step 1. Each student begins with three chips or tokens. (Chips can be made of reused materials, such as cereal boxes cut into small squares.)

Step 2. Each time individual students speak, they surrender one chip by putting it in the middle of the group or by giving it to a groupmate who acts as banker.

Step 3. When students have used all three of their chips, they cannot speak, gesture, or otherwise communicate again until all their groupmates have surrendered all their chips.

Step 4. When no one has any chips left, everyone gets back three chips, and the process begins again.

Step 5. The group discusses the pattern of interaction shown by the chips. Did one or more groupmates use up their chips quickly? Did others always seem to be the ones left with chips when others had none?

One variation on Talking Chips is to allow those group members left without any chips to ask questions to encourage their less talkative group-mates to use up their chips.

Web of Talk

Step 1. Each group begins with a ball of yarn. The person who speaks first holds the ball, wraps the beginning of the yarn around a finger, and passes it to the groupmate who speaks next.

Step 2. Group members continue speaking and passing the yarn, always wrapping some yarn around a finger before passing the ball.

Step 3. After 5 to 10 minutes, the group stops and examines the web of talk shown by the yarn. Has each person had the yarn an equal number of times? Do certain group members tend to speak before or after others?

Points to Consider About Talking Chips and Web of Talk

Both games can be played with a topic that the class is currently study-ing, or a topic outside class content can be used. One point to keep in mind is that talk is most likely to be equal if everyone is familiar with the topic being discussed.

Figure 6.1   Talking Chips is a CL technique that encourages equal participation. Students surrender a chip every time they speak. When they have used all their chips, they cannot speak again, except to ask questions, until all their groupmates have surrendered their chips as well.

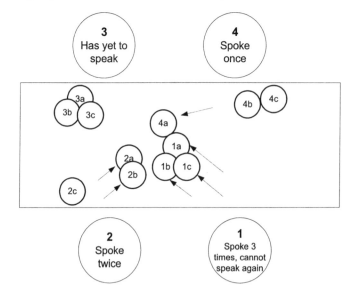

Neither Talking Chips nor Web of Talk takes into account the amount of time used in a talking turn. For instance, one student could take a 2-minute turn before giving up a chip, while another uses up three chips with a total speaking time of 20 seconds. Thus a variation on Talking Chips could be used in which each chip is worth a given amount of talking time.

MULTIPLE-ABILITY TASKS

Equal participation represents just one aspect of the larger issue of equality in groups. The Program for Complex Instruction (PCI) at Stanford University (see Resources for their Web site address) has done pioneering work on this. The people who run the program talk about the problem of status differences in groups. Status differences can result when some group members are seen as the *bright* ones, the ones in the know who are always helping the *dim* ones. This problem is exacerbated when academic status combines with ethnicity or social class. (Of course, status is a complicated issue, involving more than just academics.) Differences in status among groupmates manifest themselves in several ways, such as

- Less talk by low-status members
- Ignoring or otherwise undervaluing the contributions of low-status members
- Lack of attention and involvement by low-status members
- Hurt feelings and misbehavior by low-status members

Status differences can impede the learning of all group members. They also deprive the group of potentially useful input from members whose ideas are not respected by others.

How Do Roles Help With Status Differences?

When students with lower status exercise leadership effectively, peers' perceptions of them change, and their own self-perceptions change as well. For instance, a tendency exists for fewer female students to be given or to seek leadership roles. One way to change this is by helping females to exercise authority in their CL groups.

Researchers at PCI have developed multiple-ability tasks to address these status differences. *Multiple intelligences* (Gardner, 1993) is a term roughly related to multiple abilities. The key concept lies in the belief that

- There are many ways to be smart and many abilities that are useful for learning content.
- Within any group of people, there are differences in who is currently stronger in particular abilities, for example, who is better at drawing and who prefers to use particular abilities, such as acting in role playing.

- Most classroom activities use a limited range of ways to be smart, mostly verbal and logical-mathematical abilities.
- Tasks that use a wider range of abilities allow a wider range of group members to learn and to be the star of the group and the helper of others.

Among the features of multiple-ability tasks are these:

- More than one solution is possible.
- A variety of skills and learning formats are used.
- The task is challenging.
- Real-world, complex concepts and skills are involved.

An Example of a Multiple-Ability Task

Students study the effects on people and other species of the migration of peoples from Europe into areas inhabited by Native Americans. To learn about one example of this migration, students can participate in activities that allow them to learn from one another and build on their own strengths in a variety of areas. They can

- Listen to songs from people of different cultures (musical-rhythmic)
- Look at architectural drawings of the people's dwellings (visual-spatial)
- Read first-hand accounts of how societies functioned (interpersonal)
- Examine and use objects used in daily life (bodily-kinesthetic)
- Investigate the flora and fauna of that period (naturalist)
- Compare themselves to people from that time (intrapersonal)

To present their work, students can also use a wide range of abilities. For instance, they can

- Draw (visual-spatial)
- Create crafts and perform skits (bodily-kinesthetic)
- Grow plants from that historical period (naturalist)
- Write journal entries telling about the reactions of various people (verbal-linguistic)
- Perform songs (musical-rhythmic)

Without an emphasis on equal participation, this task about migration might have involved a lot of library reading (nowadays, supplemented by the Internet) and then writing a report. Even if students worked in a group, one or two group members who were the best at reading and writing would probably have ended up leading the group and always being the helpers.

By using a multiple-ability task, we make it likely that at one time or another, everyone in the group will be helping and, at another time, getting help. For instance, one student is best at singing while another is best at drawing, and neither is a top reader or writer. As noted earlier in this chapter, those stronger in particular areas should be helping the others get better, not doing all the work themselves. Teachers play an important role by helping students appreciate the multiple-ability nature of the task and by encouraging students to help one another develop a wide range of talents.

Many CL techniques can be used that emphasize abilities other than, or in addition to, the verbal and the logical-mathematical. Students need to:

- Understand that people have strengths in many different areas even if they have not often done well at school
- Realize that people can develop strengths in new areas
- See how various tasks require a range of abilities
- Appreciate that these abilities are distributed among their group members
- Welcome everyone's contribution as the best way of accomplishing the group's goals

To make multiple-ability tasks work toward helping all group members involves a change of mind-set. As Baloche (1998) urges, teachers need to "learn to look for what students can do rather than to look for what they cannot do" (p. 53). Students need that same outlook when working with their groupmates.

COOPERATIVE LEARNING TECHNIQUES INVOLVING MULTIPLE ABILITIES

There are many ways to make CL tasks into multiple-ability tasks. Right from the start, because every CL task is a group task, students have opportunities to use and build their skills at working with and understanding others. The next three techniques illustrate other ways that CL tasks can involve multiple abilities.

Music as Content Carrier (Jensen, 1998)

Music can promote learning in many ways. One way is by having songs carry content.

Step 1. Groups brainstorm key terms, information, and concepts from a teacher presentation, textbook section, or other source.

Step 2. Group members choose a well-known tune. Possibilities include a traditional tune, such as a folk song, or a song that is currently popular.

Step 3. Groups write new lyrics for the song taking the terms, information, and concepts from step 1 and combining them with the tune from step 2 to make a new song.

Step 4. Groups perform their new piece for another group or the entire class.

We can encourage individual accountability and equal participation by introducing these ideas:

- Groups use Circle of Speakers to brainstorm in step 1.
- Each group member writes an equal share of the lyrics of the new tune.
- All group members participate in singing their song.
- Each student performs the song for a different group, as in Jigsaw (Chapter 3).

Variations on Music as Content Carrier include students using the same procedure to create their own raps, poems, and chants instead of songs.

Group Mind Mapping

Mind maps (Buzan, 1994) are one of the most popular types of graphic organizers, along with their cousins, concept maps and word webs. Mind maps combine drawing, words, and the use of spatial relations to depict concepts and information relationships. A group mind map can be created in the following manner.

Step 1. The group begins with the central concept written as a word and image in the middle of the page.

Step 2. Each group member takes a turn to identify and draw the main ideas related to the central image.

Step 3. Group members continue taking turns to add other ideas that spring from, and connect to, the main ideas. In addition to using words and images, students use different colors and sizes of letters to make the group mind map more understandable and memorable.

Step 4. Students display and, perhaps, explain their group mind map to another group or the entire class.

Ways to promote equal participation and individual accountability when students collaborate on Group Mind Mapping or on other graphic organizers include these ideas:

- Individual pupils do their own mind maps before combining ideas with the group.
- Each pupil is responsible for one section of the mind map.
- Each pupil has a different color pen or crayon, and all the colors must be represented in the group's final mind map.
- The group uses a modification of Talking Chips, which could be called Writing Chips. Every time individual pupils write something on the map, they give up a chip. When they have no more chips, they cannot write again until all groupmates have used up all their chips.

Draw–Pair–Switch

This CL technique is one of the many variations of Think–Pair–Share, discussed in Chapter 3:

Step 1. After reading something in the textbook, listening to the teacher, viewing a Web site, or consulting another resource, each student does a drawing to represent a key idea. (The term *drawing* should be interpreted broadly to include a wide variety of visual representations.)

Step 2. In pairs, students take turns to show and describe their drawings to a partner who asks questions and gives feedback. Alternatively, the partner can be the one who starts the discussion, giving an interpretation of the drawing, after which the student who did the drawing tells what was intended.

Step 3. Group members can make changes to their drawings based on the partner's questions and feedback.

Step 4. Students switch partners and explain their former partner's drawing to their new partner.

COMING ATTRACTIONS

This chapter offered ideas on how we teachers can strive for equal participation in cooperative learning groups. Often, the tools suggested for fostering equal participation involve structuring the way that students work in their groups, such as giving students a procedure to follow, as in the steps of Draw–Pair–Switch.

Another route toward more effective group functioning involves teaching students skills they can use to work together well, skills such as asking for help, encouraging others to participate, and listening attentively. The focus of Chapter 7 is, therefore, the principle of Collaborative Skills.

7

Principle: Collaborative Skills

KEY QUESTIONS

- Is it necessary to teach students how to cooperate?
- Can students learn collaborative skills while learning content, or does it have to be done separately?
- How might cooperative learning help students develop thinking skills?

COOPERATIVE LEARNING TECHNIQUES INTRODUCED IN THIS CHAPTER

- SUMMER
- Question-and-Answer Pairs
- Tell/Rephrase
- Tell/Repeat
- Tell/Spin Off

COLLABORATIVE SKILLS

As Cohen (1994) puts it, "It is a great mistake to assume that children (or adults) know how to work with each other in a constructive collegial fashion" (p. 39). A big part of knowing how to work together is having the skills needed to collaborate with others. Look over this short list of collaborative skills that we might want to help our students develop.

- Apologizing
- Asking for feedback
- Asking for help, clarification, examples, explanation, and repetition
- Checking that others understand
- Compromising
- Disagreeing politely
- Encouraging others to participate
- Getting a group back on task
- Giving reasons
- Helping a group stick to a time limit

- Offering suggestions
- Persuading others
- Praising others
- Providing examples
- Speaking quietly
- Summarizing ideas
- Taking turns
- Thanking others
- Using humor to help group functioning
- Using people's names when speaking to them
- Waiting patiently
- Interrupting appropriately
- Listening attentively

Why Spend Time Teaching Collaborative Skills?

Some teachers might stop reading right here and say, "Yes, my students need help with collaborative skills, but I don't have time to teach them." Indeed, not every approach to CL includes explicit instruction in collaborative skills, although most do. Based on our experience, the time spent teaching collaborative skills is more than made up by the time saved when groups work well. In the short run, we are taking time to save time in the long run. Furthermore, as we tell students when we explain why we are using CL, "Knowing how to work with others is an essential life skill." It is also important to note, as you will see in the examples in this chapter, that time spent teaching collaborative skills is not necessarily time away from content. The two can be easily combined.

How to Teach Collaborative Skills

There are many ways to help students learn collaborative skills. One important way is for the teacher to explicitly model collaborative behavior. For instance, to teach the skill of disagreeing politely, we should model that behavior when we disagree with students and others.

Also, it is probably best to teach skills one at a time. We choose what skill to teach based on its immediate usefulness to students and on our appraisal of the current state of pupils' skill, ability, and use of collaborative skills. Johnson and Johnson (1998) suggest a 6-step method for teaching collaborative skills. The sample activities shown here are just a few of the many possibilities for implementing the steps.

Step 1. Students understand the need for the collaborative skill.

- Telling about our own experiences, positive and negative, with the skill
- Asking students for their experiences, in and out of the classroom
- Using a third-person experience from a story or real life, ideally, from material they are studying
- Creating a situation to help students experience why the skill is important. (For instance, to help students appreciate the value of the collaborative skill of asking for help, we can give confusing directions and ask students to follow them; as a result, either no one will be able to do the task properly or someone will ask for help in understanding the directions.)
- Having students choose the skill they want to focus on based on their own experience working in groups

Step 2. Students understand what the collaborative skill entails.

For example, if the desired skill is listening attentively, we can work with students to construct a T-Chart (for an example, see Table 7.1) that shows what the skill looks like (gestures, facial expression, posture) and sounds like (words or other sounds, written in language students might use). The T-Chart table can be posted on a wall or written on the board.

Listening Attentively

Along similar lines, students can learn set phrases for particular situations. For example, set phrases that go with the skill of disagreeing politely include

- "Good point, but have you ever considered . . . "
- "You may be right. On the other hand . . . "
- "I'm sorry, but I don't agree."
- "Let's consider another point of view."

Reading stories or showing video clips in which the skill is used also helps, as does modeling the skill by ourselves or with students.

Step 3. Students first practice the collaborative skill in isolation from class or subject content.

This involves activities in which students concentrate on just the collaborative skill. The activity is not connected to the content area we are teaching. In this way, students get a chance to really focus on the targeted collaborative skill. Examples:

Table 7.1   Attentive Listening

Looks Like	*Sounds Like*
Eye contact Nodding *etc.*	"I see." "That makes sense." *etc.*

Role plays. These can involve positive and negative examples of the collaborative skill being, or not being, used.

Games. For instance, if we are focusing on the skill of asking questions, students could play 20 Questions.

Step 4. Students practice the collaborative skill while learning class and subject content.

When students do a group activity, they make a conscious effort to incorporate the skill. One way to do this is for students to take on roles (Chapter 6), such as Checker and Conflict Creator, that involve various collaborative skills. Students can also use a variation of Talking Chips (Chapter 6) in which the chips relate to a particular collaborative skill, such as encouraging others to participate or asking for help.

Step 5. Students discuss their use of the collaborative skill.

During or after a group activity, students take time to discuss how often and well they are using the specific collaborative skill that we have focused on. To provide data for this discussion, one student per group can serve as observer. Observers note how often group members use a skill and, perhaps, what they say or do in using it. Some of the keys to successful discussion are allowing sufficient time for it to take place and setting clear expectations as to the purpose of the discussion.

The teacher can play an important role as an observer. The teacher's presence helps to remind the students to use the skill; when we aren't around, they are likely to forget. Remember, initially, to expect students to use the skill in an artificial way. Such initial artificial use of the skill is normal human behavior. It takes a while for any new skill to feel natural.

In the discussion of their use of the skill, students can talk about its use by the group as a whole, by one or more of their groupmates, or by themselves. Thus students can do group, peer, or self feedback. Younger students can indicate what they observed by circling a happy or sad face; or giving a thumbs-up, thumbs-down, or thumbs-sideways signal. Students can also use ratings scales or questionnaires, such as the one in Table 7.2.

Being specific—saying what someone actually said or did—provides better feedback than general comments. For instance, instead of a general statement, such as, "You did okay at praising others," the observer could say something like, "I liked how you disagreed politely with me by first paraphrasing what I said before giving your own view."

In addition to focusing on a specific collaborative skill, students can discuss the overall functioning of their group and its individual members. They can talk about what they did well, where they need to improve, and what actions they

Table 7.2 Rating-Scale Questionnaire

I did a good job of checking that others understood:

Strongly Disagree_____ Disagree_____ Not Sure_____ Agree_____ Strongly Agree_____

One thing that _____ (name of groupmate) did to check that others understood was _____.

Our group checked that all the members understood by _____.

can take to collaborate more effectively in the future. Having this discussion during, rather than at the end of, a group activity may be particularly useful, because students can immediately apply what was discussed.

Step 6. We persevere in helping students develop the skill.

We can't expect that after only one day, students will come to appreciate the value of a particular collaborative skill, become proficient in its use, and add it to the repertoire of group behaviors. Thus we need to persevere in encouraging students to learn and use the skill in a natural, not artificial, way.

Ways to keep the skill on students' minds include

- Classroom displays, such as posters, of collaborative skills
- Student reports on their use of the skill outside class
- Notes to parents
- Focus on the skill by administrators and other teachers
- The whole school focusing on the same skill
- Continued focus on the skill over a period of time
- Inclusion of the language involved in using the skill in the language arts curriculum
- Introduction of literature or nonfiction works in which the skill appears

THINKING SKILLS

Collaborative skills overlap with thinking skills in at least two ways. First, we think more creatively in a secure environment where we feel free to take risks. Collaborative skills, such as praising others, disagreeing politely, and listening attentively, promote an atmosphere in which students feel they can experiment and play with ideas, an atmosphere in which students build on one another's ideas rather than trying to tear them down.

A second overlap between collaborative skills and thinking skills lies in the fact that many collaborative skills—such as giving reasons, providing examples, and summarizing—involve higher-order thinking. This is where a lot of the excitement in CL comes from and where the power of the group really pays off. Yes, CL can help students remember facts and formulas, and the more knowledgeable students can share information with groupmates and help everyone get ready to do well on a test. And, yes, that basic knowledge, such as what features distinguish a spider from an insect, is important. But the real thrill of using CL with our students comes from seeing a group emerge with a new understanding, an understanding that none of the group members had to begin with. In this way, CL becomes a lot more than peer tutoring (as valuable as that is) and stimulates groups to rise to a level above that of their strongest member.

Using CL to Promote Thinking Skills

There are many ways to combine CL with other means of promoting thinking skills. For instance, research suggests that visual organizers improve thinking. Types of visual organizers include mind maps, Venn diagrams, word webs, and a variety of tables and charts, such as pro-and-con charts, which list the advantages or strong points of a concept on one side and the disadvantages or criticisms on the other side. These visual organizers can be integrated into group activities, bearing in mind the CL principles.

For teachers to help groups rise to a higher level of thinking, we need to consider how student interaction is structured and the skills students have. For instance, are students asked to explain to one another, to think aloud as they work, or to brainstorm? Do they have the necessary skills to perform these acts?

TECHNIQUES THAT ENCOURAGE COLLABORATIVE SKILLS

SUMMER

One CL technique that promotes thinking collaboratively goes by the acronym SUMMER: Set the mood; Understand by reading silently; Mention key ideas; Monitor; Elaborate; Review. The technique is slightly adapted from one developed by Hythecker, Dansereau, and Rocklin (1988) and colleagues at Texas Christian University. Here's how this pair technique works:

Set the mood. The pair sets a relaxed yet purposeful mood. They can engage in a little chitchat and also make sure they are clear on the procedure to follow.

Understand by reading silently. A reading passage (or section from a textbook) has been divided into sections. (The teacher can do this or students can use natural breaks in the passage, such as chapter sections, to divide it.) Each student reads the first section silently.

Mention key ideas. Without looking down at the text, one member of the pair acts as recaller, summarizing the key ideas of the section. Comprehension difficulties can be raised here.

Monitor. The partner looks at the text and acts as monitor, pointing out any errors, omissions, or unnecessary information in the recaller's summary and praising the recaller for a job well done. The roles of recaller and monitor reverse for the next section.

Elaborate. Both students elaborate on the ideas in the section. Types of elaboration may include the following:
– Connections with other things the students have studied
– Links between the section and students' lives

- Additions of relevant information not included in the section
- Agreements or disagreements with views expressed
- Reactions to the section, such as surprise, gladness, and anger
- Applications of the ideas and information
- Questions about things not understood or questions sparked by the section

Not all types of elaborations are relevant to every section. Groups repeat the understand, mention, monitor, and elaborate steps for all the sections of the passage.

Review. The pair combines their thoughts to summarize the entire text.

Clearly, SUMMER involves many thinking skills. We wouldn't expect students to be good at these skills right away, although it is surprising how many students seem much better at using them in nonacademic contexts. Thus we need to provide guidance before expecting students to be effective in SUMMER. Also, pay attention to the difficulty level of the texts used; how can students summarize and elaborate on a text that they can't understand?

Here is one high school teacher's experience with SUMMER:

What I did was to pair students so that, as far as possible, one was slightly stronger than the other. Then I explained the steps to SUMMER and started them on task, with the passage divided into four sections. Set the Mood was not a problem. In fact, I had to monitor this, as they were getting overly excited about setting the mood and started talking about where they should be going for lunch!

When they finally started on the UMME sections of the task, I noticed that some of the weaker students were a little intimidated by the whole task, as they felt a little pressured to understand the text and explain it to their stronger counterparts. However, as the task continued, they warmed up to the whole process as they realized that their stronger partners were able to help them through the passage when they did the monitor part of the process. The elaboration step also proved a little daunting to the weaker students, but I had told them to take turns to give elaborations, where the first student suggested an elaboration, then the other student suggested another, and so on and so forth. In this way, the weaker students also seemed a little less intimidated, and the stronger students didn't have the opportunity to take over the discussion.

Question-and-Answer Pairs (Johnson & Johnson, 1991)

Students create their own questions and answers (see Figure 7.1) and then compare them in a 2-step process.

Figure 7.1 Question-and-Answer Pairs helps students learn how to ask thinking questions. In step 1, students begin by writing individual questions and answers for themselves. Students exchange questions—but not answers—and answer each other's questions. In step 2, the pair compares answers to arrive at a final answer that is better than either of the initial answers.

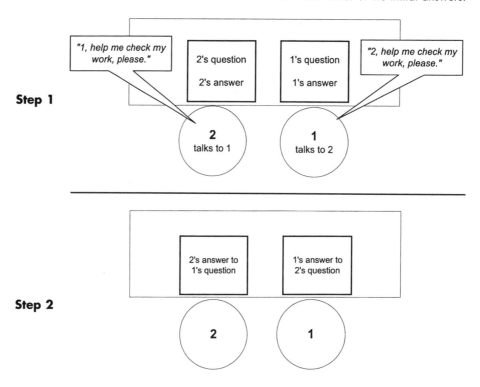

Step 1. Both members of a pair write questions. These can be of many types, including review questions or questions about content currently being studied. This is a good opportunity to help students learn how to ask thinking questions. Students write answers to their own questions. Students exchange questions—but not answers—and answer each other's questions.

Step 2. Students compare answers. Part of this comparison involves stating the evidence for their answers. As in Focused Discussion Pairs (Chapter 4), the ideal is for the students to agree on an answer that is better than either of their initial answers—proving that two heads are better than one.

A variation on Question-and-Answer Pairs is for two pairs to work together in the same way that the two partners work together. First, each pair prepares questions and then writes answers to their own questions. To encourage individual accountability and equal participation, individual members of each pair write their own questions and answers before showing them to their partner. Then the pair decides on the best questions and answers. Next, the two pairs exchange questions and create answers to the other pair's questions. Finally, the pairs compare their answers.

Just for fun, occasionally have the students exchange answers and then try to guess their partner's question as in the game Jeopardy.

Tell/Rephrase (Mid-Atlantic Association for Cooperation in Education, 1998)

When the authors of this book ask teachers for a short list of the collaborative skills they most wish their students would acquire quickly, many teachers mention the collaborative skill of listening attentively. One aspect of this skill is paraphrasing. Tell/Rephrase is a CL technique that builds this skill.

Step 1. One member of a pair makes a statement about the material being studied ("The painter tried to make this painting more serious by putting in all these shadows.")

Step 2. The other member of the pair paraphrases the partner's statement and then responds to the first statement with a related statement. ("Shadows make a painting darker and more serious. I think it's interesting how the artist also put the sun over in the corner so that it's not all dark, but the shadows still set the mood.")

Step 3. This pattern of statement–paraphrase–statement–paraphrase continues back and forth for several minutes. One sign that it is time to end the activity is that students' comments start to get off topic.

Step 4. The teacher calls on individual students at random to share something that their partner said and their own restatement of it.

Students should check the accuracy of their partner's paraphrase. If the paraphrase is incorrect, perhaps the paraphraser wasn't listening carefully, but it may also be that the speaker needs to state ideas more clearly. Paraphrasing links closely with the skill of summarizing. Indeed, a variation on Tell/Rephrase could be Tell/Summarize.

Tell/Repeat (Mid-Atlantic Association for Cooperation in Education, 1998)

This is the same as Tell/Rephrase except that instead of trying to paraphrase, students attempt to repeat what their partner said. This may be easier for students who are less proficient. In addition to encouraging students to listen attentively and speak clearly, Tell/Rephrase and Tell/Repeat also fit with the collaborative skill of disagreeing politely. We may be more willing to accept that someone disagrees with us if that person first shows that he or she has been listening to what we said, rather than just waiting for a chance to speak.

Tell/Spin Off (Mid-Atlantic Association for Cooperation in Education, 1998)

This technique promotes lateral thinking.

Step 1. The first member of a pair states an idea or names a topic.

Step 2. The other student makes a statement that connects to the first statement or topic.

Step 3. Each groupmate continues taking turns to spin off from what the partner said.

Step 4. The teacher calls on individual students at random to share some of their spin-offs with the class.

Examples of Tell/Spin Off

Language Arts
- Student #1: *Charlotte's Web.*
- Student #2: Spiders.
- Student #1: The itsy-bitsy spider went up the waterspout.
- Student #2: Mary had a little lamb. [Another nursery rhyme.]
- And so on.

Mathematics
- Student #1: $2 + 2 = 4$.
- Student #2: $4 - 3 = 1$.
- Student #1: $1 \times 17 = 17$.
- And so on.

Science
- Student #1: Lead is denser than water.
- Student #2: Water is less viscous than honey.
- Student #1: Honey is sweeter than milk.
- And so on.

Social Studies
- Student #1: Communities use resources.
- Student #2: Water is an important resource. The supply of water depends on rain and snowfall.
- Student #1: Weather patterns strongly influence how cultures develop.
- And so on.

Variations Upon Variations

As with Think–Pair–Share (Chapter 3), there are many other possible variations that we can create from the Tell/_____ beginning. Some of these modifications include

Tell/Disagree: Student #2 disagrees with student #1's statement.

Tell/Exemplify: Student #2 gives an example of what #1 said.

Tell/Generalize: Student #2 makes a more general statement from what student #1 said. For example, if #1 says, "I planted an oak tree yesterday," #2 could say, "You planted a tree yesterday," to which #1 could respond, "I planted a herbaceous plant yesterday," and so on.

COMING ATTRACTIONS

Knowing and using collaborative skills help students create powerful groups that can accomplish a wide variety of tasks. These groups share some of the roles that used to be performed exclusively by teachers. How students can move into these roles and what this means for the changing role of teachers in cooperative classrooms are issues discussed in Chapter 8, which explores the principle of Group Autonomy.

8

Principle: Group Autonomy

KEY QUESTIONS

How can I help groups become more independent of the teacher?

How much should I intervene when students are working in their CL groups?

What is the teacher's role when students have become more autonomous?

KEY COOPERATIVE LEARNING TECHNIQUES INTRODUCED IN THIS CHAPTER

Group Investigation

Paired Writing

GROUP AUTONOMY

Autonomy, the focus of this chapter, is the third universal human need described by Deci and Ryan (1985). Autonomy might at first seem to be the opposite of cooperation. However, autonomy is best conceived of not as individuals being on their own but as having power over their own fate.

Cooperative learning activities can give students some of that power. As Cohen (1994) puts it:

> Groupwork changes a teacher's role dramatically. No longer are you a direct supervisor of students, responsible for insuring that they do their work exactly as you direct. No longer is it your responsibility to watch for every mistake and correct it on the spot. Instead, authority is delegated to students and to groups of students. They are in charge of insuring that the job gets done, and that classmates get the help they need. They are empowered to make mistakes, to find out what went wrong, and what might be done about it. (p. 103)

Thus we don't rush in to save the day whenever groups face difficulties. Instead, we refine the learning environment so that students can be more self-directive. That is what we mean by the principle of Group Autonomy. For instance, we use the Team Then Teacher (TTT) technique explained in Chapter 1.

This chapter suggests ways that CL groups can have more autonomy. Perhaps some teachers feel their students are not ready for this because they are just beginning to learn CL techniques. Fine. Students, and their teachers, need time to grow accustomed to, and skilled at, student–student interaction. If you feel your students are not yet ready for more autonomy, please use this chapter as a source of ideas to keep in mind as you gradually prepare students to be more self-reliant.

So, how much teacher intervention should there be?

In classrooms where group autonomy is not being promoted, the teacher is often continually monitoring students to check their understanding of the task and the content. In the CL classroom, the teacher is also continually monitoring—monitoring how well groups, and their individual members, are functioning and learning. When students seem confused or off task, and we feel the need to intervene, we can try to

- Ask questions of the groups that stimulate their thinking.
- Provide feedback on what the group has done so far and suggest what they need to do next (see *sponge activity* in Chapter 11).
- Encourage students to use the particular collaborative skill that we have been focusing on (Chapter 7).
- Deal with status problems, for example, by giving specific, objective praise for what a low-status student has been doing (Chapter 6).
- Comment on other aspects of group functioning, for example, on how a group is going about a task and how much progress they have made.
- Promote student reflection and evaluation of what they have done.

Promoting Self-Reliance

All CL activities do not give pupils the same amount of power. Picture this scenario: We ask our students to do Circle of Speakers (Chapter 4), we assign the topic, we give a time limit, and we tell students whether their responses are right or wrong. While students may have a bit more autonomy in this scenario than if we did the same activity in a teacher-centered way, calling on one student at a time, they do not have a great deal more power.

In deciding on how much power to offer students, we need to think about our goals as educators. Many teachers list goals such as helping students become lifelong learners and encouraging a democratic spirit. These goals cannot be achieved if we always lecture to students and if we make all the decisions about what and how to learn. Just as we help students to be literate and numerate by providing opportunities for them to read, write, and calculate, so, too, can we help students to be life-long learners and active citizens by providing opportunities for them to follow their curiosity and to participate as active members in a democratic community of learners.

Some people fear that group activities will result in students going from control by their teacher to control by their groupmates, with a kind of group-think being produced. This is not what CL should be about. As stated in Chapter 6 on equal participation, the goal of the group is not the group product but the development of each individual member of the group. In the same vein, the principle of individual accountability (Chapter 4) encourages individual students to make their own unique contribution to the group based on an understanding of what the group is doing and how the group is doing it, rather than following mindlessly. This fits with the concept of a democratic community of learners, mentioned in the previous paragraph.

If we are to foster autonomy by offering more power to students, we need to trust that students can work things out with their partners. When we see groups floundering, we feel a tremendous urge to intervene, and students often expect us to do so. We may want to resist that urge. Let's show students that we have faith in the power of the group. Let's be willing, even, to allow groups to fail, in the hope that upon reflection, they will learn lessons from these failures and become more self-reliant as a result. Also, it's important to keep in mind that a certain level of conflict among students isn't necessarily bad. Conflict can be engaging and push students to think more deeply.

Scaffolding

The preparation we provide students plays a crucial role in the success or failure of CL. *Scaffolding* increases the chance that groups will succeed. Creating scaffolding can involve the following:

- Building on the skills or knowledge developed in one lesson as the class moves on to the next, so that lessons overlap and students feel capable and confident, yet are continually doing higher-level work
- Providing guide-on-the-side support as students go about tasks
- Preteaching concepts, information, and techniques to use in assigned tasks
- Providing completed examples of similar tasks
- Demonstrating how the task might be done
- Supplying prompts
- Teaching collaborative skills
- Reminding students of resources they can use, for example, reference books and electronic tools

An Example of Scaffolding in a Language Arts Lesson

The following example shows how Louisa Leong, a first-grade teacher, used several types of scaffolding (observed teaching in Temasek Primary School, Singapore, April 23, 2001, by George Jacobs).

Students were going to use Think–Pair–Square (Chapter 3) to discuss whether they liked swimming and why or why not. Ms. Leong was going to begin by using Circle of Speakers on the topic of swimming. But first, she demonstrated the technique with a student, using the word *breakfast*. During the demonstration, she showed students how to give clues if their partner had difficulty thinking of what to say. In this way, she supplied an in-context example of a collaborative skill. Next, she had a pair of students demonstrate Circle of Speakers with yet another word, *clothes*. Again, Ms. Leong intervened to show how to give help. Only after these two demonstrations did the groups do Circle of Speakers. During that activity, the teacher provided still more help, showing the class a picture of a scene at a pool to help them generate vocabulary.

Students generated many words about swimming while doing Circle of Speakers. Ms. Leong wrote these words on the board, adding a few that students had not mentioned but that she thought would be useful in the upcoming Think–Pair–Square task. She then asked a student, Aisha, if she liked singing and why or why not. The teacher wrote Aisha's answer on the board and helped the class construct a template for answers to questions, such as

I like _____ because _____.

I don't like _____ because _____.

This served as a prompt during the Think–Pair–Square activity.

Part of the art of teaching lies in deciding just how much scaffolding to provide for our students. Students new to group activities may not trust the process, may lack the skills necessary to collaborate, and may give up too easily. Therefore we may want to be sure that we provide a great deal of support for initial group activities and make sure the activities are challenging but not so challenging that the students lose confidence. As suggested in Chapter 2, we should play to success.

The use of roles (Chapter 6) offers another means of giving students more responsibility for what takes place in the classroom. For instance, when students play roles—such as Questioner, Sound Hound, and Checker—they are doing what teachers do in teacher-fronted classrooms.

WHAT IS THE TEACHER'S ROLE WHEN STUDENTS HAVE BECOME MORE AUTONOMOUS?

Okay, so we've helped the students become more autonomous. Have we thus made ourselves unnecessary? Instead of being replaced by computers, will we be replaced by our own students? Definitely not, although, as stated above, with CL, our students do take on some of the roles we used to play, and they join us in other roles, such as assessing student work (Chapter 9). Critical, ongoing roles for the teacher in a CL lesson include

- Modeling a cooperative spirit
- Preparing the ground for cooperation via the various ideas described in this book's previous chapters
- Providing a context for the lesson and the connection to prior and future learning
- Helping students understand and define the task
- Checking that students have the knowledge and skills to do the task—or the resources to acquire more knowledge and skill
- Observing student interaction
- Intervening to help individuals or groups having difficulty
- Providing closure to the lesson
- Integrating what was learned in the activity into future learning

Teaching is categorized as a helping profession, and teachers often feel a great temptation to intervene immediately to help students who are having difficulty, whether the difficulty involves understanding a concept, performing a task, or working with groupmates. However, as Dishon and O'Leary (1998) point out, by intervening, "We deny students the opportunity to learn from failure and from each other. In addition, we often overload ourselves as teachers to the point of exasperation or 'burnout'" (pp. 18–19).

Observation of Individuals and Groups

Observing lies at the heart of teaching. Teaching entails observing students' current level and adjusting instruction to help them reach the next level. In observing lessons that include CL, we focus on two broad areas—how well students are learning the content of the lesson and how well the groups are functioning. This second area relates to step 5 in the 6-step procedure for teaching collaborative skills (Chapter 7). When observing, we want to try to highlight what students do well, rather than solely focusing on shortcomings.

Table 8.1 is a sample of an observation guide and is based on a hypothetical science class studying fauna and flora and doing a Jigsaw (Chapter 3) activity in groups of four. You can use this guide to record observations of individual students in terms of their learning of the content as well as their contribution to the success of the group. A similar guide can be used in other subjects.

Sticky-Note Observations

Another technique for quickly assessing both individual and group work is to carry a clipboard and one pack of blue sticky notes and one pack of yellow. When we observe something about an individual, we write a comment on a blue note; when we observe something about a group, we write it on a yellow note. We can use the notes to make comments in general about the groups, and either to confer with individuals right then about their performance or to put into folders or files that we keep on individual students for later reference.

Intervening Through Questions

Intervening may best be done sparingly and gently. One gentle way to intervene in student groups can be via questions. Successful intervention questions get students back on task and focused. Some useful questions include:

- How did you get that answer? (process)
- Are you sure that is correct? (confirmation)
- What is your evidence? (reasons)
- What's another possibility? (alternatives)
- Why did you do it that way? (justification)
- Are you using the collaborative skill we have been focusing on? (group functioning)
- How do you think you're doing? (self-monitoring)

Table 8.1   Cooperative Learning Observations

Date:	Lesson: Fauna or Flora?	CL Technique: Jigsaw
Group: Rainbows	**Focus on the content**	**Focus on the group**
Ron P.	Got most of it	Good support to others
Yasuo M.	Good grasp of key ideas	Getting restless
Paula S.	Needs more time	Becoming more social
Kim L.	Needs review	Helpful
Paul C.	Ready to move on	Trying to stay in touch with group, but getting bored

So that students learn to integrate this sort of questioning into their interactions with their peers, you can post the most useful questions on the wall for easy reference. In addition to questions, praising offers another gentle intervention method. Specific praise can highlight the process the group is using, the effort they are making, and the fruits of their labors.

Closure

Because of time pressure, we often end lessons without leaving any time for closure. CL offers some ways to include closure. In keeping with the student-centered spirit of CL, this closure is not achieved by teachers going over the main points of the lesson, although this also can be built in. Closure in a CL lesson is best achieved when students share with each other what they have learned. One simple way to do this is a variation of Write–Pair–Share (Chapter 3).

Step 1. Each member of a pair writes two to five main ideas that they have learned and one question that they still have.

Step 2. Partners compare their main ideas and questions. They try to improve on their descriptions of main ideas and try to answer each other's questions.

Step 3. The teacher calls on students at random to share what their pair discussed.

PROJECTS

Group Investigation (Sharan & Sharan, 1992)

Another means of increasing student autonomy comes via inviting greater student input into what they learn and how they learn it. Group Investigation, described below, offers one way that students can have such input into shaping projects that they carry out. (This may be best done after students already have experience using CL.) Input from pupils can be a useful tool to help us better understand how CL is working. Furthermore, it fits well with the 5th step in the process of teaching collaborative skills (Chapter 7), in which the class discusses how well groups are functioning.

Group Investigation, developed by Sharan and Sharan (1992), involves students working together on projects. The class functions as a group of groups.

Step 1. The whole class works on one overall theme—for example, pollution—with each group investigating one aspect of pollution or sources of pollution in a particular area of their community.

Step 2. Students can work in teacher-assigned heterogeneous groups, or groups can form based on interest in the same subtopic.

Step 3. Each group decides how they will conduct their investigation, assigns tasks to the members, and completes the tasks.

Step 4. Groups plan and carry out presentations of their findings to the whole class.

Step 5. Evaluation is done by other groups, groupmates, self-evaluation, and teachers. (See Chapter 9 for more on assessing projects.)

Paired Writing (adapted from Johnson & Johnson, 1986)

Projects often involve writing. This cooperative learning technique offers a structured way for groupmates to help each other with their writing. At the same time, Paired Writing (Figure 8.1) fosters individual accountability.

Step 1. Students choose, or are assigned, a writing topic and the format—for example, a report or a narrative. Each student in the pair will create their own piece of writing.

Step 2. Members of the pair take turns telling each other what they plan to write. They contribute to each other's writing by brainstorming, asking questions, and offering suggestions.

Step 3. Students work alone to do research on their topic. Partners, as well as people from other pairs, share if they find information or ideas relevant to someone else's topic.

Step 4. Students write outlines for the text they are preparing to write. Partners provide feedback. Students create a first draft from their outlines.

Step 5. Partners provide each other with positive and negative feedback on the drafts. The focus is on the content of the draft, not on the quality of the writing. Students redraft.

Step 6. This process of draft–feedback–redraft repeats as many times as necessary. When the content seems okay, feedback focuses on the quality of the writing, for example, grammar, punctuation, and formatting.

Step 7. On each student's completed piece of writing, the writer is named as author and the partner as editor.

FURTHER OPPORTUNITIES FOR STUDENTS TO DEVELOP GROUP AUTONOMY

Service Learning

Service learning is not a CL technique. Rather, it supplies a particularly good context for cooperation and for projects. Furthermore, service learning provides a means of extending the principle of cooperation as a value (Chapter 1) beyond the small classroom group.

Service to others by students of all ages is, by no means, a new concept. Examples of service by students include cleaning parks, visiting the

Figure 8.1 In Paired Writing, students form pairs of authors and editors. In step 1, members of each pair take turns telling each other what they plan to write (as author) and ask questions and offer suggestions (as editor) about the partner's writing. Students then work alone to write outlines and first drafts. In step 2, the partners provide each other with positive and negative feedback on outlines and drafts, repeating the draft–feedback–redraft process as many times as necessary. When they complete their two writing projects (step 3), on each writer's piece, the writer is named as author and the partner as editor.

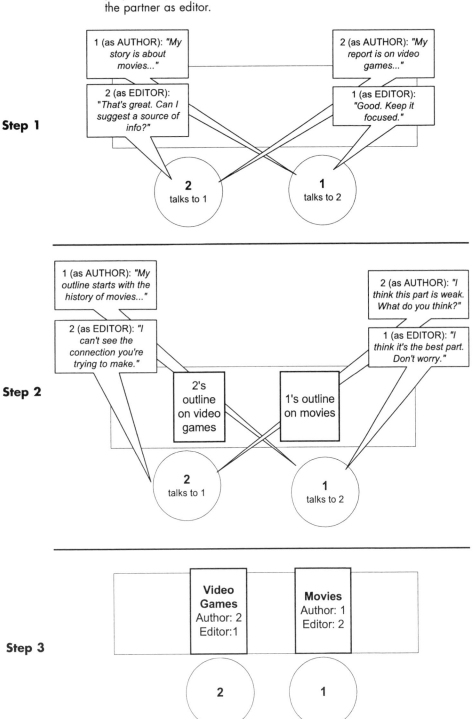

elderly, tutoring younger children, and helping the ill and handicapped. The uniqueness of service learning lies in the way it builds on these service activities by linking them with the curriculum. In this way, service projects need not be something outside the curriculum with no connection to students' academic activities. Instead, service *learning* enhances service by integrating it into students' regular course work. Service learning frequently involves students in working together. Students can collaborate at various phases of a service project in the following ways:

- Investigating the context in which the service is needed
- Deciding on which type of service will be most effective
- Identifying and exploring links between the service work and the curriculum
- Scheduling their time and assigning rotating roles to group members
- Contacting community agencies or businesses
- Eliciting parent support
- Evaluating the effect of the service they provide in order to enhance its effectiveness and identify better routes toward the same aim
- Discussing what has been learned in the course of the project
- Informing others about what has been done and learned, including follow-up contact with the community partners to thank them and let them know what the students learned from the project

Out-of-Class Academic Cooperation

When many people think of CL, they think of small groups of pupils working together in a classroom. However, CL can extend beyond the classroom. Group Investigation often involves students going together outside the classroom to conduct research for their projects. In Paired Writing, students can e-mail each other drafts and feedback. Service-learning projects normally take students beyond the classroom to help others. Students have been collaborating outside class to play sports, participate in clubs, just hang out, and, sometimes, even to study together. Indeed, university libraries often have special rooms devoted to group study.

It just makes sense that if in-class collaboration provides benefits, then out-of-class academic collaboration should as well. However, out-of-class collaboration presents new challenges, because the teacher is not around to monitor the groups.

How can we encourage collaboration beyond the classroom and enhance its effectiveness? Here is a short list of suggestions:

- Identify concepts and skills in the curriculum that suggest out-of-class learning opportunities.
- Explain to students the connection between their class work and the out-of-class activity.
- Give tasks that involve out-of-class collaboration.
- Provide or suggest places at school or elsewhere for students to do out-of-class work or research.

- Ensure that these venues comply with student needs for safety and study aids.
- Help students develop the collaborative skills necessary to collaborate effectively outside class.
- Involve parents in facilitating this collaboration.
- When students are back in class, debrief them about their experience and make explicit the ties to future learning.
- Discuss what they learned about how to work together outside class.

Letting Go and Teaming Up

Cohen (1994) sums up the teacher's role in CL as "Letting go and teaming up" (p. 103). We've already talked about how we need to *let go* and allow students to take on more responsibility. *Teaming up* means working with fellow teachers and others, such as parent volunteers and teacher's aides, to improve our use of CL. (Teacher–teacher collaboration is discussed in Chapter 16.)

COMING ATTRACTIONS

Chapter 8 concludes the presentation of eight CL principles (one per chapter) and of ideas for applying them in classrooms. However, there is still one more chapter before we go to Frequently Asked Questions (Part II). Chapter 9 deals with Assessment.

9

Assessment in Cooperative Learning

KEY QUESTIONS

How can I assess learning in cooperative groups?

What are my options for grading students, and what are the pros and cons of giving all group members the same grade?

How might I involve students in assessing themselves and each other?

How can I assess the quality of student cooperation?

THE ROLE OF ASSESSMENT

Assessment plays a crucial role in education. Education in classrooms where cooperative learning is used is no exception. However, not everything students do in their group activities can easily be assessed. For instance, measuring motivation is difficult, as is measuring whether students will be lifelong learners. Despite these difficulties, assessment in cooperative classrooms helps students, teachers, and others understand what is and is not being learned. Fortunately, we have a wide range of assessment options.

Questions That Arise

CL encourages students to help each other (positive interdependence), but this raises several questions:

If students are helping one another, shouldn't the quality of their help be reflected in their grade?

Should I assess cooperative skills along with mastery of the material?

If individual students get help completing the work, how do I assess what they learned?

Should one student's grade affect her or his groupmate's grade?

These are difficult questions, and you can probably think of many more. Although assessing CL does raise some new challenges, once we learn a few strategies, we find that we are able to find out much more about our students' capabilities and achievements than we ever were before.

Especially when implementing a new instructional strategy such as CL, it is often best not to give a grade to every piece of work a group or group member does. When students are first learning concepts or skills, their understanding may be at an early stage. Thus it may be best to wait and give them a chance to get used to working in groups for a while before grading their understanding of content and use of content-related skills.

Also, with some group products, it may be difficult to assign individual scores. In such cases, an alternative is to provide feedback on the group product but to give grades based on individually taken tests or quizzes based on key concepts, information, or skills involved in a group's product and those of other groups.

TARGET–PURPOSE–METHOD

According to Stiggins (1997), before deciding which assessment method to use, for CL or any other learning situation, teachers need to decide the target—what is to be measured; the purpose—how the information will be used; and then the method—how best to collect the information.

For example, if the target is individual student growth in content knowledge, and the purpose is to assign grades for a report card, then an individual test is probably the best method. However, if the target is the effectiveness of CL in the classroom, and the purpose is to improve how well students work together to achieve team goals, then the best method could be a measure of individual work combined with an assessment of how well the group worked together.

Remember these key terms—target, purpose, and method—when considering the assessment strategies discussed in this chapter.

CLEAR AND CONSISTENT EXPECTATIONS

Students do their best work when they know from the beginning what is expected of them and what a quality product looks like. This is true whether they are writing a story or building a model of a power plant. It is especially true when students are working in a group, as each member of the group may have a different idea about what they are expected to accomplish.

Many teachers use scoring guides to let students know how they will be evaluated on their work. Scoring guides come in a variety of forms, such as checklists showing the characteristics of good work, evaluation scales showing levels of quality, and *rubrics* (i.e., scoring guides) that clearly describe student work at each level of the scale. Three models are given later in this chapter. In some classrooms, teachers have an idea of what quality work looks like and grade based on that, but students have to guess what is "good enough," and often it seems that "just good enough" is their objective.

Today, we try to provide students with clear and consistent targets and expectations from the outset, in hopes that students are motivated to do high-quality work. Whichever kind of scoring guide or description we use, if we tell students which level of work we expect them to achieve (setting the *standard*), students are likely to work harder to meet or exceed our expectations, and they will take more pride in their final work.

Here are three options we can consider for grading the work students do in cooperative learning groups.

Option 1: Same Grade for All

Let's say that a group has done a project together. They submit their project in written and oral form, and everyone in the group gets the same grade. Reasons for adopting the same-grade-for-all option are

- Often in life, everyone either succeeds or fails together. If a business folds, everyone is out of work, regardless of each individual's contribution to that business. Conversely, if the business succeeds, even those who made less of a contribution still benefit.
- Giving everyone the same grade might motivate students to do more to help one another and to help the group as a whole.
- It may be difficult to distinguish each person's contribution to the group. After all, the teacher cannot observe all the groups all the time.

Option 2: Everyone Gets a Separate Grade

Some educators object to the same-grade-for-all view. Among their reasons are these:

- Group grades are difficult to interpret, because a student in Group A could make the same contribution to the group's project as a student in Group B, yet, if the other students in Group A are more capable and make more effort than those in Group B, the student in Group B will get a higher grade.

- Students may become unmotivated if they see their grades lowered by groupmates' poor performance.
- Group grades can become a rallying cry for opposition to CL by parents, administrators, and students.

How can we motivate students without using group grades? Some ideas are to provide

- Content so motivating that students won't need other incentives
- Nongrade rewards, as in STAD (Chapter 3), such as certificates, prizes, and applause (Rewards to hopefully avoid are those that promote non-learning-related outcomes, such as longer recess or a shorter assignment. Instead, rewards can put learning in a positive light, such as those that give more time for silent reading or for the teacher to read aloud, or that allow students to design their own assignments.)
- Goal setting by students, so that they set their own standards and develop their own ways of assessing whether they met those standards

Giving everyone a different grade is easy for a quiz or test, but not for projects. Some ways of individualizing project grades are as follows:

- Each student is responsible for one section of the project.
- Students take quizzes on the content of their group's project and, possibly, on the projects presented by other groups.
- The group part of the work, such as a group project report, is not graded, but individual parts, such as oral presentations, are graded.

Option 3: Combined Grade

Let's look one more time at the situation of a group of students collaborating to do a project. This time, rather than each student getting the same grade, each group member's grade is a combination of a group grade on the written report and an individual grade on the student's part of the oral project presentation. For instance, the written report could be worth 75 percent and the oral presentation 25 percent. If the group receives a score on the written report of 80, and Student A gets a 90 on the presentation, and a groupmate, Student B, gets a 70 for the presentation—A's grade is 82.5 ($80 \times .75 = 60 + 90 \times .25 = 22.5$) and B's is 77.5 ($80 \times .75 = 60 + 70 \times .25 = 17.5$). Or, if we are grading on a 1 to 5 rating scale, and the group score is 4, and Student C gets a 3 on the oral presentation, C's grade is ($4 \times .75 = 3$) + ($3 \times .25 = .75$) or 3.75.

The rationale for a combined grade is that it recognizes the value of the group but also recognizes differences in the achievement and effort of group members.

Combined grades can be accomplished in many ways, in addition to assigning percentages for group and individual work, as was done in the above project example. Here are a few possibilities:

- Bonus points to all group members if everyone in the group scores above a set score (exceeds standard), if all students improve on their previous scores (except for those who received very high or perfect scores), if the group's total score improves, or if the group average is above a set score
- A blend of the group's overall score with a separate score for individual group members, according to how much they contributed to the group and the level of their collaborative skills (This is one place where students can do peer assessment, because they will know better than the teacher how much each group member contributed.)

Also, to build a feeling of cooperation throughout the class, combination grades can take into account the performance of the whole class in addition to that of each group.

PEER ASSESSMENT AND SELF-ASSESSMENT

One advantage of CL over whole-class instruction is that students working in groups not only have more people who can help them, but they also have more people who see their work and can provide feedback on it. Such peer assessment (in addition to, not in place of, teacher feedback) offers many advantages:

- Teachers need to clarify assessment criteria, make them public, and help students gain skill in their use.
- By evaluating peers' work, students gain a better grasp of the characteristics of quality work.
- Students learn to evaluate their own work and internalize performance criteria.
- Students can learn from peers' positive examples.
- When students make changes based on their peers' assessments, the quality of the work reaching us is often higher.
- Peers can give each other more on-the-spot feedback because they are working side by side.

In addition to content knowledge and skills, another area for peer assessment and self-assessment is group processes. Students can assess their group, their groupmates, and themselves on how well they worked together; for instance, did they help one another? Such a focus on group interaction is one aspect of teaching collaborative skills (Chapter 7). It is critical that such peer assessment not turn into an opportunity for students to complain about their groupmates. Their comments must be constructive and focused on suggestions for how the group can better work together. The students must work together as "critical friends." For students who continue to criticize their peers, a simple list of appropriate areas on which to comment, and some discussion about constructive criticism, might be helpful.

Assessment and grading are not the same. Not all forms of assessment need to be translated into a grade. Teachers will need to decide if they want to include peer assessment and self-assessment in their grading. The same question arises as to whether to include the quality of students' collaboration as part of grades. Alternatively, some teachers give two grades, one for academics and the other for collaboration.

One factor to consider is how much we want to assign a grade to everything. The danger lies in the possibility that by using *extrinsic rewards* to encourage cooperation, we stifle the development of the spirit of cooperation as a value.

ASSESSING PROJECTS

A trend in education, seen in the increased use of projects (Chapter 8), is an attempt to connect education with the world outside the classroom. This opens the door to an exciting assessment option—having students observe the real-world impact of their work. For instance, students have monitored the water quality in a nearby stream, investigated factors contributing to the water quality, developed ways of improving it, and lobbied government, companies, and others to implement their suggestions. To evaluate their work, students can request feedback and see if their recommendations were implemented. However, implementation of recommendations is affected by myriad factors beyond students' control. Thus it might not be advisable to make grades dependent on whether a group's recommendations are implemented.

GROUP TESTS

Group tests are fairly new. In a group test, the group works together to answer the questions. Baloche (1998) proposes that such tests can come before or after individual tests. If group tests precede individual tests, they serve as a review and a chance for groups to see where their members need help. When group tests follow individual tests, they build on what students have learned in preparing for and taking the individual test.

Comparative Versus Standards-Based Assessment

Another issue to consider regarding assessment is whether to evaluate each student's work relative to the work of other students (e.g., an *A* means the best in the class) or relative to a standard (e.g., an *A* means 95 percent correct, or level 4 on a 5-point scoring guide). Although competition within the class can motivate some students, it can detract from the cooperative atmosphere in the class since by helping their groupmates learn, students may be lowering their own grade.

In order to achieve the twin goals of making expectations clear to students and promoting a collaborative atmosphere in the classroom and beyond, assessment relative to a standard of performance is often the better option. With this type of assessment, students know what is expected of them and that their grades will depend on how well they do in comparison with that standard, not in comparison with classmates. For instance, a score of 85 could be a *B*, even if the whole class scores above 85. Thus students are not penalized for helping groupmates. Everyone can get the same grade; it is not a winner-take-all situation.

Sample Scoring Guides

Table 9.1 presents a simple rubric written in language that elementary and secondary students can use to evaluate three aspects of their work—the quality of the teamwork, their own contribution, and the final product.

Table 9.2 is a rubric that covers the same aspects as the student version, but it is written from the teacher's perspective. The rubric is for teacher use, but students must know what is expected of them before they begin any work that will be assessed.

Table 9.3 is a scoring guide for assessing the use of a collaborative skill and can be filled in by making a check in the appropriate box, or the box can be filled in with a constructive comment or with a specific example (e.g., "You listen well most of the time, but not when others disagree with you.")

Table 9.1 Sample of Rubric for Student Self-Assessment of the Effectiveness of Cooperative Groups

	Teamwork	*Individual Work*	*Final Product*
1.	My team didn't work well together.	I didn't try to cooperate with my team.	Below standard
2.	My team sometimes worked well together.	I sometimes cooperated with my team.	At standard
3.	My team always worked well together	I always cooperated with my team.	Above standard

Table 9.2 Sample of Teacher Rubric for Assessing the Effectiveness of Cooperative Groups

	Teamwork	*Individual Contribution*	*Final Product*
1.	Unable to work together effectively	None of the students contributed to the progress of the team.	Below standard
2.	Occasionally worked well together but were not consistent	Some of the students contributed.	At standard
3.	Consistently worked well together with only a few lapses	All of the students contributed most of the time.	Above standard

Table 9.3   Sample Scoring Guide for Assessing Individual Student Contribution to Cooperative Groups

	Collaborative Skill: Listens Attentively		
	Approaches expectations	*Meets expectations*	*Exceeds expectations*
Barbara			
Kip			
Donna			
Rick			
Al			

COMING ATTRACTIONS

You've now completed Part I. Congratulations. Have you been trying out some of the ideas? If so, and even if you haven't, your mind is probably boiling over with questions about issues that arise when using CL. Part II considers Frequently Asked Questions About Cooperative Learning.

Part II

Frequently Asked Questions About Cooperative Learning

Research and the classroom experiences of many teachers and students indicate that collaboration among students has tremendous potential to make education a happier, livelier, and more worthwhile experience. This does not mean, however, that cooperative learning will be a big success from the beginning—twists, turns, and unexpected surprises lie ahead. Preparing for these issues equips us to deal with the ups and downs we are certain to encounter. The issues discussed in this section of the book are real ones that the authors themselves have encountered or heard about from other teachers. If these issues are not addressed, they can cause serious damage to student learning and to the cooperative environment we seek to establish via CL. However, we prefer to view these issues as challenges rather than problems, challenges that can push us toward being more insightful, more effective teachers. We believe that these challenges can be met and that CL can deliver the many advantages that collaboration offers.

The suggestions in this part of the book flow from many sources. These sources include the authors' own experiences with group activities as students and as teachers, and the experiences of their students, and of teachers whose classes they have observed and who have taken part in CL courses they have led. They also come from writers on CL, including various contributors to *Cooperative Learning* magazine (no longer in print) of the International Association for the Study of Cooperation in Education (retrieved December 31, 2001—www.iasce.org). Furthermore, a good deal of overlap exists between what is good teaching in any situation, whether or not students are working in groups, and the effective use of CL. (*Note:* The term *group* is used to refer to two or more students working together. Thus a pair is one type of group.) General education resources were also used in compiling the answers to questions in the chapters that follow.

Responses to frequently asked questions (FAQs) are intentionally eclectic, not sticking to one particular theory of learning or philosophy of education. CL represents a kind of umbrella under which educators with diverse perspectives can come together to share and debate. You are likely to find that some suggestions seem to contradict others. For example, some suggestions might reflect a view of classroom management that uses rewards and punishments to achieve good behavior, while others might reflect an approach that attempts to encourage good behavior by relying on pupils' intrinsic motivation to learn.

It is up to you to decide which of these suggestions best matches the students you teach and your learning objectives as well as your perspective on education. Please spend a bit of time reflecting on how the choices you make relate to your views of society, human nature, and education.

The questions are organized into eight chapters covering important areas:

Chapter 10 Preparing Our Classes for Cooperative Learning

Chapter 11 Managing Cooperative Learning Classes

Chapter 12 Creating CL Tasks

Chapter 13 Enhancing Thinking When Using CL

Chapter 14 Using CL in Special Situations

Chapter 15 Helping Groups That Aren't Functioning Well

Chapter 16 Collaborating With Other Teachers

Chapter 17 Working With Administrators and Parents

No doubt, you and your colleagues and students will develop still other suggestions in addition to those listed in these chapters. Please share them with the authors of this book (contact George Jacobs, gmjacobs@pacific.net.sg) and with others.

10

Preparing Our Classes for Cooperative Learning

The saying that "the devil is in the details" certainly applies to cooperative learning. Seemingly trivial matters, like how we work with students to set up the classroom, can have a big impact on student success in CL.

What size should groups be?

In this book, we have given examples of a range of group sizes, although most were groups of four and two (Chapter 2). However, there are advantages to larger groups:

- We have fewer groups to monitor.
- There are more group members to share the workload and contribute ideas.
- If each group hands in one assignment, there are fewer papers for us to evaluate.

On the other hand, the larger the group, the more skill our students need to manage the group interaction. In a pair, students only have two interactions to manage: Student #1 to Student #2 and Student #2 to Student #1. In a trio, the number of interactions that need managing goes up to six, and with a foursome, the number jumps to 12 (Johnson & Johnson, 1998).

What if there is an uneven number of students?

1. With uneven numbers, we can have one or more groups with more or fewer than four members. Strive to have as few of these groups as possible. So, in a class of 38, there could be eight groups of four and two groups of three (32 + 6 = 38), or seven groups of four and two groups of five (28 + 10 = 38).

2. If a few students are frequently absent, ask them to temporarily join a smaller group. However, try to get them into their own group soon, to help them feel like a regular group member with all the rights and responsibilities that implies.

3. When forming odd-numbered groups, continue to bear in mind the idea of forming heterogeneous groups (Chapter 2).

4. Ask an extra student to be an observer who monitors some aspect of group functioning and reports to the group or the class. However, don't leave this student in the observer role for too long.

How long should CL groups stay together?

It takes a fair amount of time to decide on the composition of heterogeneous groups. We wouldn't want to have to do that every week. However, changing group composition occasionally helps students get to know everyone in the class (Chapter 2). Hopefully, groups, in a way, will last forever, because the collaborative atmosphere engendered via cooperative learning can form friendships for life.

1. Many teachers have had success in keeping groups together for a term or half a term, a minimum of 5 to 6 weeks. This gives students time to learn how to work with their group members, thus emphasizing the importance of allotting time for groups to discuss how well they are functioning and how they can function better.

2. Being in groups that last half a term or more helps students learn to work out problems and build group identity (via group name, flag, motto, handshake, etc.); that is, they seek to develop identity positive interdependence (Chapter 3) and work on in-depth projects. Keep in mind that when groups last more than 1 day, procedures need to be in place in case students are absent.

3. At the other extreme, an informal group can exist for just 15 minutes. For example, after watching a video, students can use Circle of Speakers (Chapter 4) to discuss, and ask and answer questions about, what they just saw.

4. Long- and short-term groups can be used simultaneously. In other words, students can be a member of two groups at once. For example, students might be in one group to do a project that lasts a month but,

at the same time, be in another group for a day to work on reading skills.

5. *Base groups* (Johnson & Johnson, 1998) are groups that last at least a semester and, preferably, for a number of years. Their purpose is not to work on projects or prepare for tests. Instead, they provide support and motivation, meeting regularly to see how each member is doing in school. Base group members are like good friends which an academic focus. So, for example, if students miss class, their base group members collect the handout and homework for them.

What if students want to choose their own partners?

1. Explain the benefits of learning to work with others.

2. Allow students some input into who is in their group; for instance, students can make for-teacher's-eyes-only lists of classmates with whom they would like to be grouped, and we can try to see that at least one of these people gets into their group. Be careful with this one, because if students talk about their lists, feelings could be hurt.

3. Students can still study outside class with those whom they choose.

4. Let students know that group membership will rotate, so they will have opportunities to have many different groupmates.

How can CL work when students don't believe they can learn from their peers?

1. Students need time to know each other and an opportunity to respect the use of CL. Discuss CL with students and encourage them to consider the pros and cons.

2. Do some quick math integration—have the class calculate how many minutes a month the typical student gets to talk when the traditional teacher-fronted approach is used. This will be a very small amount. Then, they can calculate how much more student talk there is when CL is used. Isn't all that extra opportunity to be active worth the possible problems?

3. Tell them some of the key research findings, referred to in this book, that support the use of CL.

4. Let students know how you have learned from them and your past students. This encourages them to believe they can learn from one another.

5. Give your own examples of learning from peers, and ask students for their examples.

6. Show videos of CL lessons, or have students observe a CL lesson to let them see how it works.

7. Explain that CL will not be the only way they learn—sometimes, they will hear lots of teacher talk. However, CL will be used a significant amount of time, not just an hour a week for variety.

8. Students need time to know each other and have the opportunity to learn to respect the use of CL.

9. Choose familiar and favorite topics initially, so students will feel more comfortable.

10. Gradual exposure and involvement eases the transition from familiar, teacher-centered techniques to the more student-centered CL.

11. While students are in their cooperative groups, circulate among them—instead of staying at your desk marking papers—available to help groups that get stuck. This shows you aren't abandoning them.

Should anything special be done when groups end?

Yes, it's a good idea to conduct some kind of closing activity.

1. Peers can write individual or collective letters of reference for their groupmates.

2. Students can write each other thank-you notes or make statements of thanks for things their groupmates have done to make the group a valuable and enjoyable learning experience.

3. The group's work can be displayed or published as a portfolio or in another form.

4. Each group member can have some piece of the group's work to keep as a souvenir.

5. Group photos can be taken.

11

Managing Cooperative Learning Classes

Classroom management is one of the greatest challenges that teachers face. CL brings with it some potential solutions to classroom management difficulties. At the same time, it raises some special classroom management issues.

Isn't CL a recipe for chaos?

1. CL isn't magic, but years of research, as well as our own experiences, suggest that well-organized group activities, using CL principles, can actually reduce discipline problems.

2. One reason for misbehavior stems from students seeking power and more control over their learning. CL gives them more power and control.

3. Giving students more power may increase their feelings of ownership. Thus they may be more likely to see misbehavior as not just our problem but their problem as well. Peer support for prolearning behaviors can be more powerful than teacher support.

4. Because students may not be accustomed to having the power and responsibility that CL gives them, they may initially misuse

their power and avoid taking responsibility. Patience and persistence may be necessary to overcome this initial reluctance.

5. Students may respond to the new-found power that groups offer by saying, "That's the teacher's job. Why don't our lazy teachers want to do their job?" This presents a golden opportunity to discuss with students what exactly the teacher's job is and what their job is.

6. Talking out of turn represents a common misbehavior. CL greatly increases the amount of time students can talk, but this talk is (usually) on task. CL meets students' need to talk and does so in a way that promotes learning.

7. CL adds a social dimension to learning, a dimension lacking in many teacher-fronted classrooms, where talking, except when called on, is seen as off-task behavior. With CL, students enjoy a social element as part of their learning, not as a disruption to learning.

8. Students can develop their own rules for how to behave during group activities. (See Chapter 1.)

9. As Glasser (1986) put it, focusing on discipline ignores the real problem. Students will never behave well if we attempt to make them do something they don't enjoy or find too difficult. Research suggests that CL makes school more enjoyable for students, and peer support helps students succeed.

10. Students need to understand why group activities are being used. It might seem as if they are having a break during group work. In reality, groups may make them work harder, because the work is more enjoyable and motivating.

11. Tasks that are too difficult are a common cause of misbehavior. However, when students work in CL groups, they may be able to tackle tasks that were too difficult for any of them working alone.

12. As in any type of teaching, when students are off task, we need to do what Kohn (1996) proposes and ask ourselves, "What's the task?" Often, the teacher's idea of the task is not what the students think at all. This disparity includes the difficulty level and also the interest level.

13. CL groups can provide pupils with the support they need to feel comfortable taking the risks necessary to learn. People enjoy places where they feel competent and connected. CL increases the chance students will feel this way.

Should I use time limits with group tasks?

1. Time limits encourage students to use time efficiently.

2. They help students learn time management skills, especially when one student per group acts as timekeeper.

3. If the time limit is up, but most groups seem to be working well, consider extending the time limit.

Won't there be a lot of disruption and wasted time while students are moving into groups?

1. It is important to explain to the class why moving quietly and quickly is important for saving learning time and not disturbing other classes.

2. When we keep groups together for a term or so, students soon learn where they are to sit.

3. Once students know which groups they are in, tell them to be in their groups already, when the class begins, instead of having to move after class has started.

4. Just because students are seated in groups does not mean they always need to be doing a group activity. Students can still work alone, listen to us talk, watch a video, and so forth, while seated in their groups.

5. If we use CL techniques in which students move from one group to another, such as Jigsaw (Chapter 3), plan exactly how and where students should move before asking them to do so.

6. Instructions for where to move should be precise and clear.

7. If the class is large or in a confined space, ask just one part of the class to move at one time.

8. If the class will move in the same or similar ways a number of times in the course of a term, ask them to practice moving a few times, and praise those groups that move quickly and quietly.

9. Similarly, moving quietly can be a game, with the quietest groups being praised, or we can time how long it takes to get into groups and encourage students to beat their past times.

How can I quickly get students' attention when they are working in groups?

1. Time spent waiting for students to pay attention is learning time lost. Use the RSPA or another attention-getting signal (Chapter 1).

2. Explain that the attention signal is important because it saves time for learning.

3. As mentioned above, time students to see how fast they can get quiet, and get them to see if they can improve their time.

4. With young children, as an addition to RSPA, once their hand is up, ask them to point to one of their ears with the other hand. This reminds them to listen.

5. Another way to involve students in the attention signal is to clap once and have students clap twice in response to show that they are ready to listen.

6. Share ideas with other teachers who work with these students. If our colleagues use the same attention signal, students become accustomed to it more quickly.

7. In the computer lab, one thing to add to the attention signal is hands off the mouse and keyboard. In the regular classroom, also ask pupils to put down their pens and pencils.

How do you deal with groups that are too noisy?

1. Be prepared to tolerate a bit more noise as the price for having so many active students. Recognize good and bad noise. As Slavin (1995) writes, "A cooperative learning classroom should sound like a beehive, not a sports event" (p. 142).

2. Some colleagues may complain about the sound of our students talking in their groups. When you promise to help control the *noise level*, explain to them why you are using CL and how it is helping your students. This may make them more tolerant if the noise level rises occasionally.

3. Help students develop two different voices. One is used in groups. This is a 6-inch (15-centimeter) voice. In other words, a voice that can only be heard a short distance away. Some teachers refer to this as a library voice. The other voice is a class-size voice that can be heard when one student is speaking to the entire class.

4. When students sit close together, they do not need to speak as loudly to be heard. If they are sitting eye to eye, knee to knee, 6-inch voices are sufficient.

5. Along the same lines, when we keep groups small, students can speak quietly and still be heard by their groupmates, provided they are sitting close together. Thus a pair is a good size for a group that has a tendency to get noisy.

6. Ask groups to have a Noise Monitor, also known as Sound Hound or Hush Hush Captain (Chapter 6). Here are some ideas for successful use of noise monitors.
   A. Students need to learn how to be Noise Monitors. First, they need to understand why a low noise level is usually appropriate. Some reasons are to not disturb other groups or other classes; to not get sore throats; and to appear to be calm, reasonable, and polite.
   B. Next, students need to consider how some of the different ways of asking others to talk more quietly can look and sound. While this may differ from one culture to another, asking people to lower their volume could look like putting one's forefinger in front of one's lips and saying "shhhh," or moving one's hand downward, with the palm facing the floor, several times.

C. As to what asking for lower volume sounds like, students can quietly use certain phrases or gambits, such as "please speak more softly" and "could you be quieter, please."

D. To practice these gestures and gambits, students can do role plays in their groups, in which each takes a turn being a noisy student and each takes a turn being the Noise Monitor.

E. Groups can follow up on this by discussing, in their groups, how well they did on maintaining a proper noise level. For instance, they can each talk (in quiet voices, of course) about whether they ever spoke too loudly, and, if so, what caused this and how it can be remedied the next time.

7. Students may be noisy and disruptive because they do not know what to do or because they find the task too difficult. We need to help students have the necessary knowledge and skills to do the work, or know how to problem solve if they don't.

8. Many teachers have an attention signal they use when they want the class to stop talking and give their attention to the teacher. We can use another signal that says, "Please continue discussing, but do so more quietly." Here are examples that we have learned from colleagues:

- When you raise your open hand, it means, "Stop talking—attention to teacher," and when you raise your closed fist, it means, "Continue talking, but turn down the volume."
- Put a check mark on the board as the signal for students to give their attention to the teacher. An arrow facing downward is the signal for lower volume.

9. Of course, the quietest way for our students to share ideas is via the written word, either on paper or on a computer screen. Many CL techniques, such as Circle of Writers (Chapter 4), involve writing in at least part of the technique.

10. Tell students that the discussions in their groups should be their secret, for instance, when they do Question-and-Answer Pairs (Chapter 7). They can share their secrets with others later on.

What if some groups are not carrying out the task or activity properly?

1. When students try something for the first time, a certain amount of confusion is normal and can even be productive. When we use the same CL technique many times, students become familiar with it, thus reducing the need for detailed instructions. This occurs faster when our colleagues use the same CL techniques.

2. Students should understand the objectives of the lesson and how a particular task fits into the overall plan for the course, as well as how their work will be evaluated and what the criteria are.

3. Involve students in formulating the instructions.

4. Think through the instructions from the students' perspective.

5. Before students begin the activity, ask a member of the class to repeat the procedure to the whole class, or ask a member of each group to repeat it to their groupmates; for example, "Fred, you're number one in your group, right? What is going to happen after you finish interviewing Rosa, who is number four?"

6. Let students read the instructions aloud, either as a class or in their groups.

7. Give students a chance to ask questions, clarify doubts, and suggest changes to the instructions.

8. Wait until you have the students' attention before giving instructions.

9. Put the instructions on the board, a piece of poster paper, overhead projector, data projector, or handout.

10. All students should be able to clearly see us, any written directions or graphics, or any students involved in explaining the directions.

11. It may be that for some of our students, more complicated techniques can only be understood after experiencing them once.

12. When first using a new CL technique, especially one that may be a bit complicated, use content that is familiar and not too difficult.

13. Students should understand not to begin a task until the instructions are complete.

14. Give instructions in stages, so students have less to remember.

15. Demonstrate the technique by joining a group, or ask a group of students who understand the instructions to demonstrate for the rest of the class.

16. Tolerate different procedures, as long as everyone in the group is learning.

17. Monitor groups to see how they are conducting the activity. Keep an eye on groups that, experience shows, often have difficulties. If more than a few groups are confused, stop the class to explain again.

18. Stop the class to highlight one group that is working together particularly well.

19. Just as with understanding content, give students a chance to figure things out for themselves before intervening.

Is it a problem when groups finish at different times?

Not necessarily.

1. Check to see that groups that finish well ahead of the others have, indeed, really done the task.

2. If a group really has finished the task, give them a *sponge activity* or ask them to develop their own. Sponge activities soak up extra time in useful ways. The class could have a regular sponge activity, such as reading a book or working on homework, or some kind of enrichment activity on the same theme as the lesson.

3. Two groups that have finished early can compare results with each other.

4. Groups can talk about how they worked together on the task. This might provide useful information that can be shared with groups that are having difficulty.

5. Groups that finish ahead of others can help groups that are having more difficulty with the task.

6. Set time limits to encourage groups to stay on task. These time limits should be flexible. If groups are working together well but need some more time, try to give extra time.

How can group reporting be a learning experience for everyone in the class?

There are other ways for groups to report their work besides having them present to the entire class.

1. Have different groups take different aspects of the same theme. This reduces redundancy in presentations.

2. Groups can present to each other rather than to the whole class (Chapter 5).

3. Groups can exchange members to hear what other groups have done, as in Traveling Heads Together (Chapter 5).

4. Provide space—on whiteboard, blackboard, bulletin board, poster paper—for one member of each group to write their group's answer. The other members of the group can check their groupmate's work or they can compare their group's answer with those of other groups.

5. A group representative can signal their group's answer, for example, thumbs-up for agreement, or the answer can be written on a piece of paper.

6. If you do have groups report to the whole class:
   - Students hand in the work ahead of time so we can give feedback. This also helps avoid the common problem of other groups preparing instead of listening while a group is presenting.
   - Presenters can involve their classmates in their presentations, as a whole class or in groups. For instance, this can be done by using a CL technique such as Music as Content Carrier (Chapter 6).
   - As the first group presents, the other groups note the points they have made. Subsequent groups only present those points that

were not presented previously or on which they have a new slant. To avoid having all subsequent groups just say "Ditto," have them outline their points in writing before the presentations start so they can easily see what they can add to the presentation.

- Ask other students to give feedback or ask questions. This can be done in writing first.

- The rest of the class can do a postpresentation task to measure how successfully the presenters got their ideas across.

- Work with the class on the skills of presenting—staying on topic, sticking to time limits, taking into account the audience's knowledge, and using visuals to clarify and to hold attention.

- Create variety by having each member of the presenting group take a speaking part in the presentation.

- Have presenters formulate questions, either comprehension or discussion, to ask the audience. These questions can be asked before, during, or after the presentation.

How can I listen in as students are working together in their groups?

1. Pay attention to how chairs and desks are arranged so that you can easily get to all groups (Chapter 1).

2. Having the teacher join or stand near a group can have a profound effect on what is happening in that group. This can be either good or bad: good if students are off task, bad if they focus on you rather than on their groupmates. Students who are used to turning to the teacher every time they have a question will quickly revert to this when you are nearby. For this reason, it is often a good strategy to observe one group while standing next to another, nearby group. Stand or sit so that you can see and hear, but so that the students you are observing do not turn to you for help or approval. This simple technique can give you a lot of insights that you will not get otherwise.

3. When observing one group, stand or sit so that you can look up and see all, or at least many, of the other groups. For instance, when observing a group near the back of the class, position yourself in relation to that group so that you are facing the front of the class, not the back.

4. Carry a plastic chair or a light folding chair so you can sit easily, because bending down to listen in on a group, especially if students are small, may be hard on teachers' knees or inconvenient for their attire. A best-case, but unlikely, scenario is to have an empty seat in each group for the teacher.

Let students know the focus of your observations. Sometimes, it will be one or two specific things, such as the use of a particular collaborative skill (e.g., asking questions) or understanding a particular lesson objective, or it may be more general, for example, how groups are functioning.

12

Creating CL Tasks

Using cooperative learning principles and techniques, we can convert any task that students do and any activity in a textbook to a CL task. But it does take a bit of thought. As one teacher put it, "It suddenly dawned on me that cooperative learning is fun to engage in, easy to conduct, requires some additional preparation, but dynamic in outcome." Fortunately, the more experienced we are with CL, the easier this preparation becomes.

How often should I use CL?

1. Despite the research evidence supporting the use of CL, no one advocates that students always work in groups. There is still an important place for the teacher to talk and for students to work alone.

2. CL should not be reserved for every other Friday to add a little variety. Instead, it should be a regular and significant part of teaching.

3. Because many CL activities take just a few minutes, such as Circle of Writers (Chapter 4) done in pairs, it is easy to combine CL with other forms of instruction. For instance, we can explain an idea first, before students work in groups on a task related to the idea.

4. Alternatively, we can use a more inductive approach in which students first try to figure things out for themselves before we give our ideas.

How can I find the time necessary to prepare structured CL activities?

1. Although there is additional preparation involved in setting up CL activities, especially when the activity is new to the teacher and students, CL can actually reduce our workload in several ways:
   - There is less need to prepare teacher presentations to the whole class. Time preparing materials can be reduced, because there is sometimes only one handout per group rather than one per student.
   - Correcting and monitoring student work can also be easier, because students working in groups can help eliminate some problems before they get to us, and peers can give each other some constructive feedback as well.
   - Many teachers have students grade each other's papers. This is very easy to integrate into cooperative learning.

2. More and more materials are being published that incorporate CL. Look for these and for CL ideas in teachers' guides.

3. Internet sites contain ready-made CL lesson plans. Ask around and surf for ones that you like. One place to start is the Web Sites list in Resources (Part III).

4. Use non-CL activities from textbooks by just changing the directions to make them cooperative group activities.

5. Share materials and lesson plans with colleagues.

6. As with most other things, the more we do CL, the better and faster we get at it. And over the years, we accumulate lots of materials. We can reuse and modify these.

7. With time and guidance, students too get better at doing CL and can work together more independently. Involve them in some of the preparation.

How are CL lessons different from teacher-fronted lessons?

In many ways, the lessons are the same. This should be no surprise, because CL lessons often include teacher-fronted instruction. Here are some features common to the two types of lessons and the unique aspects that CL adds to the lesson:

1. **Understanding the objectives** involves helping students see (and possibly involving them in deciding) what they should gain from the lesson, how the lesson forms part of the course objectives, and how it will connect to future learning.

   Groupmates check that they all understand the objectives. They appreciate that everyone in the group needs to learn and help others learn. Besides the normal objectives, CL lessons also include objectives related to how to improve collaborative skills and group functioning (Chapter 7).

2. **Input and modeling** involves providing information and skills that will help students attain the lesson objectives, and modeling the use of this information and these skills.

   In CL groups, peers help with the input and modeling. Also, discovery methods can be used in which students gain knowledge inductively and try out skills.

3. **Practice** gives students opportunities to practice the information and skills.

   This practice can come in the form of teacher-led activities or individual work, but peers can also help one another practice, either by working together or by checking each other's individual work.

4. **Assessment** involves monitoring to see if the objectives have been met.

   Instead of the teacher being the only one doing assessment, peers can participate as well.

5. **Closure** involves thinking back about what was learned and how it was learned as well as thinking forward to how the learning can be applied and what should be learned next.

   Many CL techniques are applicable here, for example, Circle of Interviewers (Chapter 2) and Question-and-Answer Pairs (Chapter 7). Also, group functioning will be one of the topics on which students reflect.

Won't group activities take too long?

1. Remember, the point is not to cover the material but to uncover it. Thus think about covering less, with CL helping students to understand it more deeply.

2. Emphasize learning-to-learn skills. These skills can facilitate content learning in the long run, although, initially, they may slow things down as students learn them.

3. CL activities can be integrated into other modes of teaching. For example, when giving a lecture or demonstration, stop every so often for students to do a CL activity, such as Ask Your Neighbor (Chapter 4). Such activities give students a chance to consolidate and verbalize the knowledge being presented, and we get an opportunity to check how students have interpreted what has been presented.

4. Instead of each group presenting their answers or projects in front of the whole class, use CL techniques in which groups present to each other, such as Traveling Heads Together and Carousel (Chapter 5).

5. Set time limits on activities to encourage groups to get and stay on task, thus speeding up group activities.

6. Let groups delegate one member to be the Materials Manager who distributes and returns materials (Chapter 6). This can be faster than if we take the role.

Won't students complain about using the same CL technique, or even using CL, again and again?

As with any classroom activity, students may complain if they are asked to do the same thing many times, but in our experience, this happens far less often than in traditional, teacher-fronted activities.

1. The keys to making groups interesting are the same as for making any kind of school activity interesting:
    *   Engaging topics
    *   Challenging but doable tasks, for which students have the necessary preparation to succeed
    *   Tasks that students see as relevant to their needs
    *   The potential to gain a feeling of satisfaction from work done well

2. There are many variations on CL techniques. Students can come up with their own or we can suggest possibilities.

3. Using the same CL technique many times has pluses:
    *   Students get good at using the technique and feel comfortable with it.
    *   Just as with learning a new dance, once we are comfortable with the steps, we can focus more on other things, such as adding a twist.
    *   Once students master a CL technique, they can also think about whether they and their groupmates are using appropriate collaborative skills, for example, asking for reasons.
    *   Students can also spend more time discussing how their group can work together more effectively in the future (Chapter 7).

What if CL tasks are too difficult for students of different ability levels?

1. Motivate students by helping them see the importance of the task. One way to work toward this is to involve students in formulating questions and tasks.

2. Provide a framework or rubric for doing the task, such as a sample mind map (Chapter 6).

3. Break the task into smaller parts.

4. Allow more time for groups that need it. Trust that they can do the task. Emphasize that groups are not racing each other. Provide a sponge activity (see Chapter 11) for groups that have finished.

5. Do a Jigsaw (Chapter 3), in which each member of the group has part of the information. Students work with peers from other groups to learn their part well and then teach it to groupmates.

6. If students are currently in pairs, increase the size of the group, thus increasing the chance that some will have the prior knowledge or skills needed to do the activity.

7. Add more information; for example, show a video, give a mini-lecture, or do a demonstration before the groups begin their work.

8. Provide more resources, such as CD-ROMs and reference books.

13

Enhancing Thinking When Using CL

The development of students' thinking skills is high on the agenda of many teachers, and rightfully so. CL offers a fabulous venue for students to mobilize and improve their thinking skills.

How can I encourage students working in groups to show creativity or other evidence of higher-order thinking?

1. Not all students arrive in school with these skills. During content lessons, specifically teach such skills as brainstorming, analysis, and considering a variety of solutions. Students need to see the value of these skills in learning content, not in isolation.

2. Use CL techniques that include thinking skills, such as SUMMER (Chapter 7).

3. Ask questions with more than one possible good answer, and let students know that there isn't just one correct answer.

4. Help students understand that learning is a developmental process in which mistakes are to be expected and that there are rewards in trying out new ideas.

5. Promote group norms in which students aren't afraid to take risks, make mistakes, and ask for help (Chapter 1).

6. Give ample time for students to respond. Allow them time to think alone and discuss with their peers, for instance, via Think–Pair–Share or related techniques (Chapter 3).

7. After students reply to a question:
   - Don't evaluate every answer. Instead, sometimes paraphrase or summarize an answer or just acknowledge it.
   - Ask follow-up questions: Why do you say that? Could you please give an example?
   - Ask follow-up questions that require students to describe the procedure they used to get their answer.
   - Use the Socratic method by asking students to defend their answers, for example, by asking students to present and rebut a view opposed to the one they have just presented.

8. Don't be too dominant. This leads students to feel their job is just to match the answer in the teacher's mind or to regurgitate what they have been told.
   - Talk less.
   - Build on what students say, to show the value of their ideas.
   - Avoid stating your opinion in a way that may shut off debate. Instead, if stating your view, acknowledge that other views or approaches exist.
   - Discuss your own mistakes and learning journey.
   - Accept unexpected but reasonable answers.

How can I ensure that group members avoid reaching quick consensus and have richer discussions?

On the surface, this might seem to be a good situation, but too often it means that groups are not engaging in in-depth discussion.

1. Emphasize the value of diverse opinions. These quotes may be helpful:

   > If two people have the same opinion, one is unnecessary. I don't want to talk, to communicate, with someone who agrees with me; I want to communicate with you because you see it differently. I value that difference. (Covey, 1990, p. 278)

   > If everybody is thinking alike, then somebody isn't thinking.[1]

   > An enemy will agree, but a friend will argue. (Russian proverb)

   > If we never fight, how can we ever get to know each other? (Cantonese proverb)

2. Do not always require consensus, although students should be urged to work toward it. Unless we encourage students to try for consensus, they may just agree to disagree without really trying to convince one another.

3. Defend the value of minority views, not just during CL activities but in all settings. The students are always watching us for models.

4. Highlight the process rather than the result.

5. Allow sufficient time so that students do not have to rush to agreement.

6. Question whether groups that quickly reach agreement have really delved deeply into the issue. Ask them to describe how they considered other options.

NOTE

1. Quotation retrieved December 27, 2001, from www.generalpatton.com/quotes.html (© 2001 Estate of General George S. Patton Jr. c/o CMG Worldwide).

14

Using CL in Special Situations

This chapter looks at the use of cooperative learning in three teaching situations that may be a bit different from the usual classroom:

- Teaching young children
- Teaching students who are learning in a second language
- Teaching large classes

PRESCHOOL AND LOWER ELEMENTARY SCHOOL STUDENTS

Can I use CL with preschool and lower elementary school students?

Yes, CL can work with young children, and the students' later teachers will be grateful for the preparation in cooperation the children receive while young. Many of the nonacademic activities of early childhood education are good opportunities to build cooperative skills.

1. According to some of the leading child development researchers, children as young as 2 years old can understand the cognitive and affective perspectives of others.

2. CL can help young children build their awareness of others. Also, they develop their communication skills.

3. The universal human needs of relatedness, competence, and autonomy apply to young children as well. Relatedness may be especially important to children who are not yet very comfortable with being at school and away from home.

4. With young children, it is important to start by teaching cooperation as a value (Chapter 1). To do this, we:
   - Use the language of CL. If you see examples of spontaneous cooperation, for example, helping behaviors that students exhibit during play or study, tell the children that this is cooperation.
   - Encourage children to notice the many types of help that they receive, not just from family members but also from people at school.
   - Model cooperative behavior.

5. Start right away to build a cooperative environment in your class. For instance, the class can work together to
   - Plan activities
   - Welcome new students
   - Make sympathy cards for classmates who are ill
   - Clean the classroom
   - Solve problems that arise in the course of the day

6. Collaboration on nonacademic tasks, such as helping each other dress for cold weather, offers another means of fostering a collaborative climate.

7. Set aside time for cooperative play, in which adult intervention is kept at a minimum.

8. Use games in which everyone can be a winner.

9. When using group activities with preschool children, it is probably best to start with groups of two.

10. Children need to experience success in their group activities so that they feel comfortable with groups and confident that groups can succeed. In other words, students need both "I can" and "we can."

STUDENTS LEARNING IN A SECOND LANGUAGE

How do I use CL with students learning in a second language?

We can use just about all CL techniques with second-language learners, as long as the language task is within their reach. In fact, many of the ideas in this book were developed by the authors in our use of CL with students for whom English is a second language.

1. Remember that these students' low proficiency in a second language does not mean that their intellectual capacity is also low. Thus

while we may want to keep the language level low, we should use concepts appropriate to native speakers of that age.

2. These students often lack confidence. By using CL, we help them build confidence by providing a support group—a classic CL benefit. Once these students become familiar with CL techniques, the techniques boost confidence by providing structure and clear, expected outcomes. They know what to do.

3. If second-language students are also taking courses in their native language, CL can be explained and started there.

4. Make language proficiency a variable when setting up heterogeneous groups. In this way, the more proficient are right on the spot to help their less proficient groupmates.

5. In CL activities in which students take roles, start out second-language students with roles that require less language, such as Timekeeper. Then gradually move them into more demanding roles. (See Chapter 6 for more on roles.)

6. Help second-language students develop the vocabulary to understand instructions for group tasks and communicate with groupmates. (See *set phrases* in Chapter 7.) By doing this in their second language, we build language proficiency at the same time that we help groups function well.

7. These students may benefit if we give them additional preparation time by using CL techniques such as Think–Pair–Share (Chapter 3).

8. Provide more language support—for example, model dialogues, vocabulary work, and listening activities accompanied by a written version of the text—before asking such students to interact in their groups.

9. In their groups, students have opportunities to try out and modify the language they will use before speaking to the whole class or to another group.

10. In countries such as the United States, a common situation is that some students are native speakers of the language of instruction, usually English, while for other students, English is a new language. Suggestions for mixed classes include the following:
    - Multiple-ability tasks (Chapter 6) rely on other talents, in addition to English proficiency, and allow students whose English is limited to shine.
    - Lots of visual cues and other types of language support provide alternative paths to understanding.
    - In forming groups, place students who have fairly strong bilingual skills with students whose English is weak. At the same time, pay attention to whether this helping role is overburdening the bilingual students.

- Consider the fact that students may bring different cultural expectations of classroom norms or may have had little prior exposure to school. While respecting their background, work with them so that they learn the expectations of the school and classroom.

How should I respond when students use their first language in CL groups using another language?

1. Take a long-term view. These students are learning many things at the same time—a new language, a new culture, academic content—and they may be unfamiliar with collaborative group work. It is not surprising that it may take a while for them to get comfortable and confident with the second language (L2) and with working in groups.

2. Some use of the first language (L1) may be beneficial for a number of reasons. For example, some words are very difficult to explain or guess from context, and if the group has a time limit, it may be faster to use an L1 translation. Remember, we're helping students add a new language, not subtract their L1.

3. By using CL, we help to create a supportive, low-pressure environment in which risk taking, such as using the L2, is encouraged, and it is okay to make mistakes.

4. Use the L2 when walking around the room and speaking to individuals or groups of students.

5. Rather than scolding students for L1 use, praise them when they use the L2.

6. Consider whether there is sufficient language support, for example, demonstrations of appropriate language, so that students have the resources to do the task in the L2.

7. Students very likely have the habit of using their L1 when they speak to one another during class as well as outside class. We need to recognize that habits take a while to change.

8. Discuss the issue of L2 use with students, and encourage them to reach a class consensus on using the L1 in their groups.

9. Some students use the L1 because they feel uncomfortable making mistakes in speaking in front of their peers. Explain that there is a time for accuracy and a time to focus on fluency and meaning. CL activities usually focus more on the latter.

10. Suggest that one member of each group be the Language Monitor or L2 Captain, whose role is to encourage appropriate L2 use (not to discourage L1 use).

11. CL activities, such as Write–Pair–Switch (Chapter 3), provide students with time to plan how to put their thoughts into L2 words before they need to speak.

12. Through CL writing activities, we help those students who feel more comfortable writing than speaking in the L2, because there is less time pressure and no worries about pronunciation. So, if students speak in the L1 in their group, they can hand in a piece of written work in the L2.

13. Give each second-language student L1 tickets for the day, semester, or whatever, and let students decide together if they need to use the L1. They turn in a ticket each time they use the L1. You can ask the students later to discuss how many tickets they used and why. Optionally, you can give recognition to those who use fewer tickets.

14. Alternatively, give each second-language student four Talking Tokens. (This is a variation on Talking Chips, Chapter 6.) Every time they speak, they give up one token, but when they speak in the L1, they give up two tokens. When they have no tokens left, they cannot speak again until all their group members have used all their tokens.

15. Decide with students to designate one small corner of the classroom as the place where they can go temporarily to speak the L1.

LARGE CLASSES

How do I use CL with large classes?

Large classes make it even more important for us to use CL, because in a teacher-fronted mode, the larger the class, the less chance each student has to participate. Basically, CL is used the same way in large classes as in small ones. We just have more groups.

1. Groups in large classes need to learn to be more independent because we have less time to supervise each group. We need to find ways to help students be more independent, not necessarily a bad thing, but definitely a challenge. (See Chapter 8, Group Autonomy.)

2. Work with students to establish routines early in the year so that group procedures, such as moving in and out of groups, can happen quickly and quietly.

3. Do more preparation to choreograph and rehearse movements in groups. Otherwise, confusion may result. Also, make instructions very clear, because we cannot get around to every group.

4. Because large classes make it more difficult to monitor groups, we may want to spend more time helping students develop collaborative skills (Chapter 7) and more effort having students monitor their

own groups, for example, by appointing pupils to be facilitators in each group.

5. Base groups (see Chapter 10) are a great help in large classes. Use base groups to help with such matters as attendance, catching up absent or newly admitted students, and checking homework. Groups also provide a support network so that students do not feel lost in a large class.

6. Strive to reduce the feeling among students that unless the teacher sees the group present their work, the activity is incomplete. After all, teachers have other means of checking students' understanding, and teachers aren't the only source of verification. Use TTT (Chapter 1).

7. Large class size in terms of students does not always go with large class size in terms of the dimensions of the classroom. To cope in these cramped conditions, we can
   - Encourage students to sit close together
   - Keep group size small (four or fewer)
   - Use a uniform arrangement for all groups
   - Make sure there is space to walk around the room and monitor all the groups

15

Helping Groups That Aren't Functioning Well

Effective group dynamics are key to successful cooperative learning. "It is social support from and accountability to valued peers that motivates committed efforts to succeed" (D. Johnson & R. Johnson, as cited in Gibbs, 1994, p. 195). Unfortunately, there are often one or two groups that don't seem to function as well as the others. This section looks at some ways we can help such groups.

What can I do when students don't get along with their groupmates?

1. Establish guidelines and rules for how to work together (Chapter 1). Students can have a voice in establishing these.

2. Make clear your zero-tolerance policy toward impolite treatment of groupmates, such as physical or verbal abuse, put-downs, or refusing to offer assistance (Chapter 1).

3. Students may follow the teacher's lead. If we show a high level of respect for all, in time, most students will respond.

4. Do classbuilding and teambuilding activities (Chapters 1 and 2). In one such activity, students learn the names of each of their groupmates or classmates plus, perhaps, one other piece of information, such as a hobby. Later, they take a quiz to check their memory. To prepare for the quiz, students try to use their groupmates' and classmates' names as much as possible.

5. Stress that in life, we seldom get to choose whether to work alone or with others, or with whom we must collaborate. For example, we teachers don't get to choose our colleagues. Turn a negative into a plus by pointing out students' opportunity to learn to work with a wide variety of people.

6. Many high-status jobs—indeed, all types of jobs—involve working with others. For example, doctors need to collaborate with a whole team of medical personnel and also to communicate with patients and their families. CL provides students with a chance to practice this collaboration.

7. Emphasize the use of skills necessary to collaborate with others (Chapter 7). For example, we can focus on taking turns by putting a pencil in the middle of the group, and only the person holding the pencil can talk. Then, everyone else must take a turn before that person can talk again.

8. Sometimes, students find it easier to complain to you than to discuss problem situations frankly with one another. Encourage them to try to work out their own problems, and then invite disgruntled groups to make an appointment with you to discuss their difficulties.

9. Set aside time for groups to discuss how well they are functioning and to think of ways to function more effectively in the future.

10. Avoid separating students when they don't get along. Emphasize that you will not separate them until they have learned to get along. If we separate groups that do not get along, we deprive them of the opportunity to learn how to overcome initial difficulties in a group.

11. Think of ways to increase the level of positive interdependence in the groups (Chapter 3). For instance, give each group member different information and a task that requires them to share information to succeed, as in Jigsaw (Chapter 3).

12. Strengthen celebration/reward positive interdependence (Chapter 3). For instance, determine what rewards really matter to students and offer those.

13. When students each have a role to play in the group, they work together better.

14. Start with random grouping at first, to emphasize that it is just the luck of the draw who ends up in which group. Ways to randomize are as follows:
    - Count off by numbers. The formula for knowing which number to count to is to divide the number of students in the class by the

number of students you want per group. Thus if there are 40 students and you want groups of four, 40 divided by four is 10; so, students count to 10. For variety, you can count in different languages.

- In a variation on counting off, students "word off" (Johnson & Johnson, 1998). We write words on the board, for example, the names of famous scientists. The number of scientists equals the number of groups we want.

- Each student in the class can be given a card in a category, such as animals. Again, the number of different kinds of cards matches the number of groups that we want to establish. Students find members with the same card and sit together to form a group. For instance, if various animals appear on the cards, students can find their partners by imitating the sound that their animal makes.

15. Invite students to group themselves according to such criteria as birthday month, favorite color, preferred food, or favorite movie. This may help them overcome whatever makes them hesitant to work with one another.

16. Provide teambuilding activities that help students learn about each other, for example, food exhibits, artifacts, art, and music (Chapter 2).

My students argue with one another. How can I turn arguing into productive disagreement?

1. Work with the whole class to develop rules for conduct in groups (Chapter 1).

2. Teach the collaborative skill of polite disagreement (Chapter 7), and help students see the benefits of disagreement.

3. Emphasize cooperation throughout your curriculum. Cooperation is something to teach about, not just a way of teaching.

4. Ask students to paraphrase each other using Tell/Rephrase (Chapter 7). Feeling understood by another person and really trying to understand her or him often reduces arguments.

5. Assign one student the role of Facilitator (Chapter 6).

6. Record students on videotape or audiotape as an aid to their understanding their interaction.

What can I do about students who don't participate much in CL activities?

1. Make sure what happens in the CL part of the lesson is perceived by students as clearly aligned with their goals, for example, doing well on exams. All parts of a course need to fit together.

2. Use CL activities that have a game-like quality, such as Teams–Games–Tournament (Slavin, 1990, pp. 66–78) or Two Facts, One Fiction (Chapter 1).

3. Try CL activities that use a range of abilities, such as musical-rhythmic or bodily-kinesthetic (Chapter 6).

4. Encourage enthusiasm for cooperation by talking with fellow teachers and with others about how you benefit from cooperation.

What about students who really want to work alone?

1. Many group activities combine individual and group work. For instance, when a group does a project, students often research, write, and present individually. Point out to students the individual aspects of group activities.

2. Perhaps the student wants to work alone because of past bad experiences with groups. Find out about this, explain how CL addresses these concerns, and point out that CL isn't just throwing students into groups.

3. Assessment may be one reason that some students want to avoid groups (Chapter 9), for instance, if the entire group will receive the same grade. If we use this type of assessment, we should carefully explain why, and perhaps we should have a fallback option if one group member really leaves the group in a lurch.

4. Increase the difficulty, complexity, or length of a task. This helps students see that they need groupmates to succeed.

5. Remind students of the benefits of learning how to collaborate with others.

6. Use more teambuilding and classbuilding activities to create more of a community feeling within the class.

7. If the student remains adamant and is likely to be disruptive if put into a group, we may decide to let her or him work alone, with some conditions. It is very important that the student not see working alone as a reward for having complained. Here are a few sample conditions:
   - Anyone working alone does the same work as groups.
   - After working alone for a certain period of time, the student gives groups another try.
   - The student plans what to do to make subsequent entry into a group successful.

What about students who dominate their group?

Because of students' different experience, in any *particular* activity, some students will be likely to participate more or less. That's okay. What's not okay is if it is always the same students who are not participating.

1. Assign dominating students to observe group interaction.

2. Explain why everyone should participate. We can improve our ideas by trying to explain them to others. When others hear what we say, they can learn from us and also help us learn, and the group benefits from getting everyone's ideas.

3. Use Talking Chips and Web of Talk (Chapter 6), or limit each person to 20 seconds per turn. Hopefully, after doing this a few times, awareness will be raised, and students will not need these artificial constraints.

4. Each time a group member speaks, one student records who spoke. Students can also record to whom they spoke, whether to all members, to only one member, and so forth. Studying this record later gives everyone a picture of how balanced the participation was.

5. Assign roles to uninvolved students. Start with roles that match their strengths (Chapter 6).

6. Similarly, talk to students who dominate their groups. Ask them why they do not encourage others to participate.

7. Reduce group size (Chapter 2). The fewer members there are, the more likely all are to participate. In this regard, pairs are ideal.

8. Place nonparticipants in a group with at least one student who seems very good at helping and encouraging others. Show your appreciation to such students.

9. Allow planning time so students can prepare what they are going to say. One way to do this is to use activities such as Write–Pair–Switch (Chapter 3) that provide time for students to write their ideas before being asked to speak.

10. In many CL activities, each group member has unique information, for example, Jigsaw (Chapter 3). The group cannot succeed unless all members share their information.

11. Other CL activities provide each member a turn to speak, for example, Circle of Speakers and Circle of Writers (Chapter 4).

12. Give less talkative members a role that calls for talking, for example, Facilitator, and give more talkative members a role that calls for listening, for example, Recorder (Chapter 6).

13. One group member can take the role of Checker (Chapter 6). The Checker's job is to be sure that all group members can tell about and explain their group's work.

14. Teach the collaborative skills of turn taking and encouraging others to participate (Chapter 7).

15. Provide students with scripts that provide some or all of the words or set phrases they will need to use in particular situations: for

example, a card with set phrases listing the opening words students can use for a particular purpose, such as praising others or asking for reasons.

16. Create groups of all talkative and all less-talkative members.

17. Some students who aren't talkative may be more willing to write, draw, sing, mime, or participate in other ways. Tasks that call for a wide variety of intelligences help all group members have a chance to shine.

18. Pay attention to the seating arrangements. Arranging chairs symmetrically encourages everyone to participate (Chapter 1).

19. Find out why some students are not participating by talking to them alone or using dialogue journals, in which students write about their thoughts and experiences and teachers and other students write responses. Perhaps it is due to family problems, an emotional or physical difficulty, a task that is too hard or confusing, or just a problem in adjustment to working in groups.

20. Because of students' different backgrounds, in any particular activity, some students will be likely to participate more. That's okay. What's not okay is if it is always the same students who are participating more.

What can I do when less able students hurt their group's performance?

Inevitably, there will be a group in your class in which the less prepared or less able students are holding back the performance of the group as a whole. Remember that when we use CL, we have more time to spend with students who are having problems, because with CL, other students are, hopefully, engaged in learning in their groups. Further, CL increases motivation because it is no longer just the teacher trying to motivate students, but their peers are motivators as well. Thus less able students are likely to try harder.

1. Preteach these students (during recess or after school) upcoming course content so that they have information other students may not have and, thus, may be in the position of giving help rather than always receiving it.

2. Urge students to ask for explanations and urge their fellow group members to provide explanations, not just answers. Research by Webb (1989) suggests that if groupmates provide each other with answers but not explanations, neither party learns. Just passing someone the answer helps neither the recipient nor the giver (Chapter 5).

3. Use different levels of materials for different members of the group. For instance, this can be done in Jigsaw (Chapter 3). Also, see the Success for All Web site (listed in Resources) for CL techniques specifically designed for this purpose.

4. Teach the collaborative skill of asking for explanations. Quote this Malay proverb: "If you are reluctant to ask the way, you will be lost."

5. Use multiple-ability tasks (Chapter 6), because these give all students a chance to be the star of the group.

6. Find ways to motivate students to help weaker members and for weaker members to try hard to improve.

7. Felder and Brent (1996) give this advice to students complaining about being slowed down by having to explain material:

> If you ask any professor, "When did you really learn thermo-dynamics (or structural analysis or medieval history)?" the answer will almost always be, "When I had to teach it." Suppose you are trying to explain something, and your partner doesn't get it. You may try to explain it in a different way, and then think of an example, and then, perhaps, find an analogy to something familiar. After a few minutes of this, your partner may still not get it, but you sure will.
>
> In our experience, most students bright enough to complain about being held back by their classmates are also bright enough to recognize the truth of the last argument. We also point out that most students will eventually have jobs that require them to work in teams and that learning how to do so is an important part of their professional training. (p. 46)

What can I do when students give each other the wrong information?

1. Remember that understanding is usually not an all-or-nothing process. Instead, understanding comes step by step, as we gradually arrive at a fuller grasp of a concept. When we teach via a teacher-fronted mode, students also have misunderstandings. The advantage of groups is that during the group interaction, these understandings are made public, allowing teachers and groupmates to address them.

2. See the responses above to the problem of less able students. Many of those responses apply here as well.

3. Walk around while students are working in their groups. This will allow you to identify misunderstandings before they get too far.

4. If you notice that a few groups have the same misunderstanding, you might want to stop the group activity and do some whole-class teaching.

5. Encourage groups who understand to help those who do not.

6. When using a CL technique such as Jigsaw (Chapter 3), in which students teach each other, ask students to answer some questions or do drafts of their teaching presentation before they start teaching

peers. Look at their drafts to see if students are ready to teach their groupmates.

What can I do when there is cooperation within groups but not between groups?

1. Do classbuilding activities that develop a sense of class spirit (Chapter 1).

2. Each group can do one part of an overall class project, as in Group Investigation (Chapter 8). This will motivate groups to share resources with other groups.

3. Change group membership several times a year (Chapter 2), and occasionally do short activities that use random grouping so that students get a chance to be groupmates with many of their classmates.

4. Encourage groups that finish early to help others.

5. The class can compete as one to achieve a goal, for example, to attain an average score above a given standard (Chapter 3).

16

Collaborating With Other Teachers

Cooperation is not just for students. We teachers, too, can benefit from collaboration with peers. This fits with the principle of Cooperation as a Value (Chapter 1). Here are some ideas on how to share CL with your peers.

Most other teachers at my school don't seem interested in CL. Should I give up on them?

1. Perhaps the best way to convince other teachers is by example. Invite them to watch you teach using CL, or videotape a class of yours when CL is used.

2. Students can help convince other teachers. If our students appreciate the CL lessons they use in our class, they may discuss this with their other teachers. Then, if these teachers try CL, it will be easier for them, because some of their students are already comfortable working in CL groups.

3. Use CL techniques at various kinds of meetings, for example, union meetings and department gatherings.

4. Let colleagues know about workshops and courses related to CL.

5. Similarly, share books and videos (see Resources for recommendations) and other CL resources.

6. Convince administrators to use, or let you use, CL techniques in staff meetings so that colleagues can get first-hand experience with CL.

7. Be patient and remind yourself that the fact that others don't teach as we do doesn't make them bad teachers.

A few other teachers I know are using CL. How can we help each other?

1. Form a study group of teachers who work together to implement CL. Study groups can be very powerful tools for self-improvement. Explore some of the reference material in Resources (Part III) as a group. Try to meet regularly to provide each other with support, insight, and inspiration.

2. Group members can teach the same collaborative skill to their students.

3. Plan lessons together. Even if you don't teach the same course, you can still give each other feedback.

4. Each try out the same CL technique in class and report on how it worked and on any adaptations that you developed.

5. If you teach different subject areas, work together to plan coordinated units. For example, a mathematics teacher and a language arts teacher can collaborate to develop coordinated project ideas.

6. If possible, occasionally team-teach, that is, two teachers in the same class at the same time. This won't always be easy to arrange, but it's great to do!

7. Observe each other's classes and provide feedback.
   - Record a lesson on audiotape or videotape.
   - As the teacher being observed, tell the observer what aspects of the class to watch out for.
   - Hold a debriefing session afterward to compare notes.

8. Remember positive interdependence (Chapter 3), individual accountability (Chapter 4), and equal participation (Chapter 6) in your teacher group.

9. Don't forget to include teachers' aides, parent volunteers, and others in your collaboration.

What goals should my teacher support groups strive for?

1. Learn to take any lesson and introduce a CL component into that lesson.

2. Use CL as a component in more than 50 percent of your lessons.

3. Use CL techniques and concepts in your group.

4. Look for ways to connect with teachers at other schools.

5. Find ways to share CL with other interested teachers.

6. See the use of groups as a ladder with four rungs. Teacher groups can help their members and other teachers move up this ladder.
   A. Bottom rung—no use of groups
   B. Second rung—use of groups without the use of CL principles and techniques
   C. Third rung—use of CL principles and techniques
   D. Top rung—specific attention to improving the interaction in CL groups by such means as students thinking aloud, using graphic organizers, and practicing the wide range of collaborative skills that overlap with thinking skills, such as elaborating, summarizing, and asking for reasons

7. Look for ways to integrate cooperation as a value into various aspects of school life, for example:
   - Cooperation between classes
   - Service-learning projects (Chapter 8)

With what other changes in teaching does CL fit well? Why?

1. Student-centered approaches, because in CL students play a greater and more varied role in their own learning (Chapter 1).

2. Global education and values education, because coming to know, and learning to collaborate with, others toward common goals is fundamental to making a better world (Chapter 1)

3. Heterogeneous classes (Chapter 2), with learning about other cultures and seeing beyond stereotypes, because students interact meaningfully with others who are different from themselves

4. Meaning-based and interactive methods, because the quantity of student talk skyrockets (Chapter 5)

5. Teaching for multiple abilities, because CL provides opportunities for students to develop their interpersonal intelligence and other intelligences (Chapter 6)

6. Thinking skills (Chapter 7), because explaining and discussing with others sharpens our thinking

7. Learner autonomy (Chapter 8), because CL moves away from the teacher-centered classroom

8. Task-based teaching, because most tasks in real life, such as service learning (Chapter 8), are done with others

9. Learner strategy training, because many useful learning strategies require collaboration

10. Emphasis on a variety of learning styles, because CL broadens the range of teaching and learning modes

17

Working With Administrators and Parents

In addition to students and other teachers, administrators and parents (and other caregivers) are two additional key allies that we teachers have in our efforts to help learning succeed. We need to enlist these allies' support in the use of CL.

How can I respond to administrators and parents who worry that CL won't prepare students for multiple-choice tests such as the SAT?

1. Gently remind them that the shortest distance to the goal is not always a straight line; for example, research suggests that the best way to increase one's vocabulary is not to study lists of words but to do lots of reading. In other words, even though students do not take their tests in groups, maybe studying together is, nonetheless, a good way to prepare for them. It's like the scaffolding used in constructing a building. The group provides the support to prepare students to eventually stand on their own.

2. If students comprehend a concept well enough to explain it to a peer, they really comprehend it. As Einstein reportedly once said, "You haven't really understood something until you can explain it to your grandmother." Also, helping others builds self-confidence.

3. To prepare for tests, students can practice in their CL groups with past versions or practice versions of the test (or teacher-made replicas). Here are two ways:

A. Pairs of students work on 10 to 20 items at a time. Students work through the items, agree (or not) on the answers, record both answers if they differ, then check with an answer sheet that is provided after they have finished. Pairs ask other pairs for explanations on items they have missed. Any items still not understood (or also missed by the other pair) are checked with a third pair. We are consulted only as a last resort.

B. Prepare simple board games (roll the dice, move a marker) to use with test items. Cut the test items into strips, one item per strip, and put the strips in envelopes. Each group of four gets an envelope, answer sheet, game board (make one on 8½-by-14-inch paper and duplicate), and a die or spinner. The students provide their own markers (coin, eraser, paper clip). In turn, they roll the die, move their markers, and answer a question from the envelope, while another group member checks the answer sheet. A student who gets it wrong moves back to the space she or he held at the beginning of that turn. Groups will often want to discuss each item among themselves before and after checking the answer. With both this and the preceding activity (A above), it's good to have intact copies of practice tests to distribute. Otherwise, some students may want to copy each item into their notebooks.

Will CL give me enough time to cover the syllabus and finish the textbook?

1. CL may be slower at first because teachers need to learn how to use it and need to spend time incorporating it into their lessons, and students need time to learn to collaborate and become familiar with various CL techniques. However, CL is quicker and more efficient later, as students become more successful and more enthusiastic about learning and as you benefit from the additional power of many minds working together.

2. Years of research support the theory that active, student-centered learning strategies, such as CL, are much better than lecture alone for improving long-term retention, changing attitudes, improving problem-solving skills, and developing collaborative skills. Thus the long-term gain is worth the initial effort and time.

3. If the syllabus were reconceived to include objectives for lifelong learning, such as "learning to work with others," CL would be seen as an integral part of the syllabus.

4. With CL, we don't need as much repetition of points and examples of the points to provide reinforcement, because the reinforcement comes in the group activities.

5. Individualized activities can be done outside of class, for example, in the library or on a computer. In that way, we have more class time for activities that promote interaction, such as CL activities.

6. In the traditional classroom, students learn that they don't have to read the assigned materials; the teacher will cover all the important stuff anyway. With CL, we can spend class time on trouble spots and going beyond the basic facts and into application. And students face peer pressure to be prepared in order to help the group.

How can I work with administrators who do not support CL?

1. The Association for Supervision and Curriculum Development (see Resources), an international organization to which many administrators belong, produces publications that advocate CL. The ASCD journal, *Educational Leadership*, has had many articles on CL—some of the best have been published in a collection (Brandt, 1991). And ASCD has published a very good book on CL (Johnson, Johnson, & Holubec, 1993), which is also available in Spanish.

2. We can show administrators many reviews of relevant research that suggest that CL is associated with gains in learning and other variables, such as self-esteem, liking for school, interethnic relations, and higher-order thinking. This research involves studies done with students from a wide variety of age groups who were studying a wide variety of subject areas (see Baloche, 1998; Davidson & Worsham, 1992; Johnson & Johnson, 1998; Kagan, 1994; Kohn, 1992; Sharan, 1994; Slavin, 1995).

3. We can remind administrators that nowadays, many curriculum documents at various levels, from individual schools' policy documents to national curricula, advocate the use of group activities and the learning of the skills and attitudes necessary to collaborate with others (Chapter 1).

4. If administrators are concerned about the noise level in your classroom, take the steps advised (see Chapter 11), and, at the same time, help the administrator to see that all noise is not the same; the noise students make while collaborating on learning tasks is productive noise.

5. Point out that CL helps students learn how to learn.

6. Stress that schools have a responsibility to help create citizens with cooperative skills and attitudes.

7. Discuss the concept of a cooperative school, one in which positive interdependence (Chapter 3) is felt not just within groups or within classrooms but throughout the school. Good books on this topic are Johnson & Johnson (1994) and Sharan, Shachar, & Levine (1999).

8. Urge your administrators to talk to their counterparts in schools where CL use is widespread and successful.

9. Most important, invite them to watch you using CL. Successful students are the best argument for any instructional approach.

Part III

Resources for Cooperative Learning

CL PRINT RESOURCES

Baloche, L. (1998). *The cooperative classroom: Empowering learning*. Upper Saddle River, NJ: Prentice Hall.

Bennett, B., Rolheiser-Bennett, C., & Stevahn, L. (1991). *Cooperative learning: Where heart meets mind*. Toronto, Canada: Educational Connections.

Brandt, R. S. (Ed.). (1991). *Cooperative learning and the collaborative school: Readings from* Educational Leadership. Alexandria, VA: Association for Supervision and Curriculum Development.

Brody, C. M., & Davidson, N. (Eds.). (1998). *Professional development for cooperative learning: Issues and approaches*. Albany: State University of New York Press.

Buzan, T. (1994). *The mind map book: How to use radiant thinking to maximize your brain's untapped potential*. New York: Dutton.

Cohen, E. (1994). *Designing groupwork: Strategies for the heterogeneous classroom* (2nd ed.). New York: Teachers College Press.

Covey, S. (1990). *The 7 habits of highly effective people*. New York: Fireside Books.

Davidson, N., & Worsham, T. (Eds.). (1992). *Enhancing thinking through cooperative learning*. New York: Teachers College Press.

Deci, E. L., & Ryan, R. M. (1985). *Intrinsic motivation and self-determination in human behavior*. New York: Plenum.

Deutsch, M. (1949). A theory of cooperation and competition. *Human Relations, 2*, 129-152.

Dishon, D., & O'Leary, P. W. (1993). *A guidebook for cooperative learning: A technique for creating more effective schools*. Holmes Beach, FL: Learning Publications.

Dishon, D., & O'Leary, P. W. (1998). *A guidebook for cooperative learning: A technique for creating more effective schools* (2nd ed.). Holmes Beach, FL: Learning Publications.

Dumas, A. (1998). *The three musketeers.* (Lowell Bair, Trans.) New York: William Morrow. (Original work published 1844.)

Felder, R. M., & Brent, R. (1996). Navigating the bumpy road to student-centered instruction. *College Teaching, 44,* 43-47. Retrieved June 6, 2002, from http://www2.ncsu.edu/unity/lockers/users/f/felder/public/Papers/Resist.html

Forest, L. (2001). *Crafting creative community: Combining cooperative learning, multiple intelligences, and nature's wisdom.* San Clemente, CA: Kagan Publications.

Gardner, H. (1993). *Multiple intelligences: The theory in practice.* New York: Basic Books.

Gibbs, J. (1994). *Tribes: A new way of learning together.* Santa Rosa, CA: Center Source Publications.

Glasser, W. (1986). *Control theory in the classroom.* New York: Harper & Row.

Grineski, S. (1996). *Cooperative play in physical education.* Champaign, IL: Human Kinetics.

Hythecker, V. I., Dansereau, D. F., & Rocklin, T. R. (1988). An analysis of the processes influencing the structured dyadic learning environment. *Educational Psychologist, 23,* 23-37.

Jacobs, G. M., Gan, S. L., & Ball, J. (1997). *Learning cooperative learning via cooperative learning: A sourcebook of lesson plans for teacher education.* San Clemente, CA: Kagan Publications.

Jensen, E. (1998). *Teaching with the brain in mind.* Alexandria, VA: Association for Supervision and Curriculum Development.

Johnson, D. W. (1989). [Leader, cooperative learning workshop]. Honolulu, Hawaii.

Johnson, D. W., & Johnson, R. T. (1986). Computer-assisted cooperative learning. *Educational Technology, 26,* 12-18.

Johnson, D. W., & Johnson, R. T. (1991). *Cooperative learning lesson structures.* Edina, MN: Interaction Book Company.

Johnson, D. W., & Johnson, R. T. (1994). *Leading the cooperative school.* Edina, MN: Interaction Book Company.

Johnson, D. W., & Johnson, R. T. (1998). *Learning together and alone* (5th ed.). Boston: Allyn & Bacon.

Johnson, D. W., Johnson, R. T., & Holubec, E. J. (1993). *Circles of learning* (4th ed.). Edina, MN: Interaction Book Company.

Johnson, D. W., Johnson, R. T., & Smith, K. (1991). *Active learning: Cooperation in the college classroom.* Edina, MN: Interaction Book Company.

Kagan, S. (1994). *Cooperative learning.* San Clemente, CA: Kagan Publications.

Kagan, S. (1998, September). [Leader, cooperative learning workshop]. Presented by Singapore Teachers Union, Singapore.

Kearney, P. (1993). *Cooperative learning techniques.* Hobart, Tasmania: Artemis Publishing.

Kohn, A. (1992). *No contest: The case against competition* (2nd ed.). Boston: Houghton Miflin.

Kohn, A. (1996). *Beyond discipline: From compliance to community.* Alexandria, VA: Association for Supervision and Curriculum Development.

Luvmour, S., & Luvmour, J. (1990). *Everyone wins! Cooperartive games and activities.* Philadelphia: New Society Publishers.

Mid-Atlantic Association for Cooperation in Education. (1998, September). How to use the "scripts" menu in an ESR (every student response) classroom. *MAACIE Cooperative News,* pp. 7-10.

Orlick, T. (1978). *The cooperative sports and games book: Challenge without competition.* New York: Pantheon.

Orlick, T. (1981). *The second cooperative sports and games book.* New York: Pantheon.

Palmer, P. J. (1993). *To know as we are known: Education as a spiritual journey.* San Francisco: Harper.

Palmer, P. J. (1998). *The courage to teach: Exploring the inner landscape of a teacher's life.* San Francisco: Jossey-Bass.

Patton, G. S., Jr. © 2001 Estate of General George S. Patton Jr., c/o CMG Worldwide. Retrieved December 27, 2001, from www.generalpatton.com/quotes.html

Ruddock, J. (1978). *Learning through small group discussion.* Guilford, UK: Society for Research into Higher Education, University of Surrey.

Sapon-Shevin, M. (1999). *Because we can change the world: A practical guide to building cooperative, inclusive classroom communities.* Boston: Allyn & Bacon.

Sharan, S. (Ed.). (1994). *Handbook of cooperative learning methods.* Westport, CT: Greenwood Press.

Sharan, S., Shachar, H., & Levine, T. (1999). *The innovative school: Organization and instruction.* Westport, CT: Bergin & Garvey.

Sharan, Y., & Sharan, S. (1992). *Expanding cooperative learning through group investigation.* Colchester, VT: Teachers College Press.

Slavin, R. E. (1990). *Cooperative learning: Theory, research, and practice.* Englewood Cliffs, NJ: Prentice-Hall.

Slavin, R. E. (1995). *Cooperative learning: Theory, research, and practice* (2nd ed.). Englewood Cliffs, NJ: Prentice Hall.

Stiggins, R. J. (1997). *Student-centered classroom instruction* (2nd ed.). Upper Saddle River, NJ: Merrill.

Webb, N. M. (1989). Peer interaction and learning in small groups. *International Journal of Educational Research, 13,* 21-39.

WEB SITES

1. Association for Supervision and Curriculum Development (ASCD)

If you go to the site and do a search for *cooperative learning,* you find a lot of good information, including articles from *Educational Leadership.*

Retrieved December 27, 2001, from www.ascd.org

2. Centre for the Study of Learning and Performance

The Centre is a research centre at Concordia University, Montreal, Canada. Their goal is to study and promote effective teaching and learning strategies through active association with schools, administrators, and teachers, particularly in the areas of cooperative learning and integrated technology.

Retrieved December 23, 2001, from doe.concordia.ca/cslp/Try.htm

3. CLUME (Cooperative Learning in Undergraduate Mathematics Education)

The Mathematical Association of America's Project CLUME is a program for mathematics instructors at all postsecondary levels who are interested in using cooperative learning in their mathematics classes. The site contains an electronic newsletter, math texts suitable for cooperative learning classrooms, 10 guidelines for students doing group work in mathematics, suggestions for designing and giving cooperative learning workshops, and responses to a survey on cooperative learning.

Retrieved December 23, 2001, from www.uwplatt.edu/~clume/

4. Cooperative Learning Center at the University of Minnesota

The Center offers research updates, a question-and-answer section, and many publications and other materials on CL. Codirectors: Roger T. Johnson and David W. Johnson.

Retrieved December 23, 2001, from www.clcrc.com/

5. The Cooperative Learning Network

The Cooperative Learning Network is an association of colleagues at Sheridan College, Ontario, Canada, who model, share, support, and advocate for the use of cooperative learning. It includes the TiCkLe Guide (Technology in Cooperative Learning); retrieved December 27, 2001, from www.sheridanc.on.ca/academic/edserv/TCL.htm

Retrieved December 23, 2001, from www.sheridanc.on.ca/coop_learn/cooplrn.htm

6. Educational Resources Information Center (ERIC)

If you go to this site and search for *cooperative learning*, you will get enough hits to keep you busy for a while.

Retrieved December 29, 2001, from searcheric.org/

7. Richard Felder's Homepage

Richard teaches engineering at North Carolina State University. Lots of good stuff here related to CL.

Retrieved December 26, 2001, from www2.ncsu.edu/unity/lockers/users/f/felder/public/Cooperative_Learning.html

8. Hong Kong Cooperative Learning Center

The Center works with universities and schools throughout Hong Kong as well as in China and elsewhere in Asia. Their Web site includes their newsletter and publications by scholars associated with the Center. Principal investigator: Dean Tjosvold.

Retrieved December 23, 2001, from www.ln.edu.hk/hkclc/

9. Cooperative and Collaborative Learning Page of the Centre for Enhances Learning and Teaching at the Hong Kong University of Science and Technology

Provides practical advice for teachers at the university level who want to use CL. Features a video of an overview talk on CL by David Johnson of the Cooperative Learning Center at the University of Minnesota.

Retrieved May 20, 2002, from celt.ust.hk/ideas/ccl/

10. Instructional Innovation Network: Cooperative Learning in Higher Education

This site offers resources, including essays and lesson plans, for post-secondary-level educators.

Retrieved December 26, 2001, from www.bestpractice.net/ FMPro?-db=null.fp5&-format=/CLHE/CLHE.htm&-view

11. International Association for the Study of Cooperation in Education (IASCE)

The leading networking organization on cooperative learning.

Retrieved December 23, 2001, from miavx1.acs.muohio.edu/ ~iascecwis/

12. George Jacobs's Homepage

Go to the CL section for a number of articles on CL.

Retrieved December 23, 2001, from www.georgejacobs.net

13. The Jigsaw Classroom

This site contains information on Jigsaw, one of the oldest and best-known cooperative learning techniques. Among the features of the site are Jigsaw's history, a description of how to implement the technique, troubleshooting ideas, a list of books and articles about Jigsaw, and information on recent, related work by Eliot Aronson, one of the originators of the technique.

Retrieved December 23, 2001, from www.jigsaw.org/index.html

14. Pete Jones's Home Page

Pete is Head of Modern Languages at Pine Ridge Secondary School in Ontario, Canada, and presents cooperative learning strategies that he and others developed.

Retrieved December 26, 2001, from www.geocities.com/Paris/ LeftBank/3852/cooplearn.html

15. Kagan Cooperative Learning

This site offers a newsletter, a question-and-answer section, workshop information, and the chance to buy lots of material on CL and related topics by Spencer Kagan and his colleagues.

Retrieved December 26, 2001, from www.kaganonline.com

16. Mid-Atlantic Association for Cooperation in Education (MAACIE)

This organization promotes CL in the U.S. mid-Atlantic region. The site includes articles from MAACIE's newsletter.

Retrieved December 23, 2001, from www.geocities.com/~maacie/

17. National Institute for Science Education (NISE)

The NISE's collaborative learning page (college level one) features stories by university lecturers who use collaborative and cooperative learning, plus lots of useful tips, explanations of a variety of techniques, responses to FAQs, and a list of resources.

Retrieved December 29, 2001, from www.wcer.wisc.edu/nise/CL1/CL/default.asp

18. Program for Complex Instruction (PCI), Stanford University

This site features the work of Elizabeth Cohen, Rachel Lotan, and their colleagues who have focused on the sociology of cooperative learning groups, in particular, the treatment of status differences among group members.

Retrieved December 23, 2001, from www.stanford.edu/group/pci/

19. Ted Panitz's Homepage

Ted teaches mathematics at Cape Cod Community College in West Barnstable, MA. His page includes two e-books, one on CL and one on writing across the curriculum. Also included are some of the wide-ranging Internet discussions that Ted has put together across several lists.

Retrieved December 23, 2001, from home.capecod.net/~tpanitz

20. Success for All Foundation (SFAF)

SFAF is a not-for-profit organization dedicated to the development, evaluation, and dissemination of proven reform models for preschool, elementary, and middle schools, especially those serving many children placed at risk. Cooperative learning is a key component of their model. The organization was founded by Robert Slavin and his colleagues.

Retrieved December 23, 2001, from www.successforall.net/

Index